Otto, the Boy at the Window

OTTO, THE BOY AT THE WINDOW

Peter Otto Abeles' True Story of Escape
from the Holocaust and New Life in America

Peter Otto Abeles
and
Tom Hicks

CREATIVE ARTS BOOK COMPNY
Berkeley • California

For information contact:
Creative Arts Book Company
833 Bancroft Way
Berkeley, California 94710
1-800-848-7789
www.creativeartsbooks.com

ISBN 0-88739-375-6
Library of Congress Catalog Number 2001095279

Printed in the United States of America

We dedicate this book to
Jean and Jerome Abeles
and
Leah and Theodore Abeles
who responded to the distant cries of despair
thereby saving Peter Otto and his family
from imminent death and ultimately
making this book a reality

Foreword

When Tom Hicks and I met some fifteen years ago, neither of us understood the significance of that meeting and how we would be drawn to telling the story of my life. Our backgrounds are so different, but our friendship transcends the boundaries of culture and time.

We have attempted to relate a personal story of triumph over tragedy, of love over fear, and, above all, of forgiveness. While the Holocaust is an important historical event that affected the lives of millions of people, it can best be understood by describing in detail how an individual was impacted. Concurrently, we then examine the mindset of a small child who is faced with the transition from a wealthy European setting to a working class neighborhood on the south side of Chicago. Most importantly, we attempt to reconcile a man with the haunting past of a frightened boy caught up in a tumultuous, seemingly loveless relationship with his parents. We believe that this mix provides an entertaining and introspective viewpoint that will instill a ray of hope to a world surrounded by violence and fear.

Shalom!
Peter Otto Abeles

TABLE OF CONTENTS

Chapter I

"No one can make you feel inferior without your consent"

Chapter II

"Things do not get better by being left alone"

Chapter III

"The highest wisdom is loving kindness"

Chapter IV

"Life is a series of surprises"

Chapter V

"You must be the change you wish to see in the world"

Chapter VI

"I'm a great believer in luck, and I find that the harder I work, the more I have of it."

Chapter VII

"If you judge people, you have no time to love them"

Chapter VIII

"Love...is a living reality"

Chapter IX

"The mystery of life is not a problem to be solved, it is a reality to be lived."

Chapter X

"Not I — Not anyone else, can travel that road for you. You must travel it for yourself"

Chapter XI

"In the beginner's mind there are many possibilities, but in the expert's there are few."

Chapter XII

"Thoughts are things"

Chapter XIII

"All the world loves a winner, and has no time for a loser"

Chapter XIV

"It's been a hard day's night, and I've been working like a dog"

Chapter XV

"The block of granite which was an obstacle in the path of the weak becomes a stepping stone in the path of the strong"

Chapter XVI

"What I have lived through I know. What I am going to live through only God knows."

Chapter XVII

"As Love enters, fear vanishes"

Chapter XVIII

"Relax. Listen. God is with you right here, right now"

Chapter XIX

"Dignity does not consist in possessing honors, but in deserving them."

Chapter XX

"We must laugh at man to avoid crying for him."

Otto, the Boy at the Window

CHAPTER I

"No one can make you feel inferior without
your consent."
Eleanor Roosevelt

Have you ever had the feeling that someone was watching you? I was having that feeling today. I had been sitting on my bed when I stood up and casually walked to the massive window of my hotel room, and as I pushed the sheer white curtains aside, observed the traffic below from my seventh floor perch. I wiggled the toes of my bare feet and cinched the belt of my terry cloth robe. I looked up and found that I felt as safe here as the group of sea gulls must have felt circling above quietly observing the world below. I loved looking out windows of any size with any view; it did not matter now, nor had it ever mattered. I had been a watcher all my life and saw no reason to cease this perfectly fulfilling pastime. It was a warm sunny day in late May, and this part of Long Island was so pretty this time of year bursting forth in spring colors. This was an important day for me. Today I would bury my mother, Karla, and quite possibly some ghosts from my past. I sidestepped to the mirror positioned next to the television and observed myself. I looked none the worse for wear, though my eyes looked a little tired. Tan, fit, incredible me I thought to myself. "It's all in the marketing" an old friend once told me.

Anyway, my name is Peter Otto Abeles and at sixty-eight years of age, I have concluded that the things I have tried hardest to forget are ultimately the things I am destined to remember. It's more than slightly ironic I suppose; but nevertheless, those dangerous, frightening years of my youth occupy the same position in my mind that manifests itself in the body of a cool, confident adult, the patriarch of an American family.

1

I spent the whole morning, and oh what a morning it was, with Rabbi Mellman, a new acquaintance, who, by the way, would be handling the funeral service. That it was called a "service" seemed a bit odd to me. I quite succinctly relayed some critical facts to him about my mother's life; and later while standing at the graveside, I could hear his words that were actually my words repeated back to me and the others in attendance with a dirge-like cadence. He was a nice young man with a beautiful voice but the words sounded hollow for the first few minutes. Then Rabbi Mellman spoke of forgiveness, the blessings of God, and of the sacredness of life. These spiritual terms were simply theories to me, not realities in my life. I squeezed my wife Bonnie's familiar hand and I thought to myself, "How many people really knew my mother or me?" What words can possibly summarize a life or express a relationship? Words could not begin to do it. I knew it all too well. However, throughout my entire adult life I had sought to complete things because incomplete puzzles were not acceptable to my mother or me. Then it occurred to me that somehow during the remainder of my life I must put together those fragmented pieces of my past that have shaped me, sometimes quietly without my knowledge; and other times when I screamed and openly fought against them. I felt the urge to act quickly and end the confusion as painlessly as possible though my gut told me this was unlikely. If I could make everything fit neatly and logically together, I might somehow reconcile these conflicting emotions that I have. Strangely, I seem to be experiencing relief and freedom rather than the expected feelings of sorrow and love. Guilt, however, did surround me like the burial shroud that now clothed my dead mother. I wondered how she might be feeling at this moment. That suddenly seemed like a weird thought, probably a mental "red herring" to divert attention from myself. My mind then repeated that this way of thinking is wrong, but my heart retorted that it is absolutely right. I wondered if I was losing my mind. At least, that would be an acceptable excuse, one that I could clearly explain after shock treatment or drugs. I turned and snatched my travel bag from the bed and retrieved the tie case. Perhaps I could lose myself in an important decision such as the color and pattern of an appropriate neckpiece. This Armani seems to be perfect; we must look our best at times like this.

Twelve hours that seemed like an eternity had passed and I found myself staring out the same hotel window again that evening. The traffic below looked the same as before. I closed my weary eyes for a moment and remembered a time when the boy, me, Otto, was staring out the window many, many years ago.

* * *

I must have leaned too close to the windowpane for my warm breath had fogged the glass. I took my shirtsleeve and wiped across the pane until the fog was removed. Ahh… I could see through again, but at the same time I was able to look outside I could see a shadowy reflection of myself as well. I amused myself by blinking, pursing my lips, and wriggling my nose. This person I could learn to love. It was harder to accept the person that I saw in the mirror of my bathroom, positioned below a bright light, a light that revealed every flaw. I don't know when I became self-conscious, but it was clear to me that others expected a great deal of improvement in order for me to be acceptable. I could only stand brief periods of this self-examination so I turned quickly to look out the window again.

It was a typical cloudy March day in Vienna, Austria. For days, the adults around me had seemed apprehensive and I knew something was amiss. Nothing unusual seemed to be happening in the street, then, without warning, the peaceful calm was broken by loud shouts and cheering. I turned my head sideways to see a throng of people marching down my street. It was almost like a celebration. Nazi flags like I had seen in my father's newspaper began to appear in the windows across the street from our apartment. Unbeknownst to me, loudspeakers had been attached to the lampposts on the street and they began to blare with a loud, high-pitched voice. I didn't know it at the time, but the voice was that of The Fuhrer himself, Adolph Hitler proclaiming The Anschluss, the annexation of Austria to the Third Reich. The latest nightmare had begun but nobody living in the city in the mid-1930s knew just how badly it would develop. That world outside my window was beyond my understanding. My greater concerns lay within these four walls of brick, mortar, plaster, and wood where the fear was far more personal...far more painful.

I continued to watch with the remnants of dried tears on my seven-year-old cheeks while my arms were aching as never before. Today at lunch my beautiful mother Karla was insistent on my holding heavy books under my arms in place during the entire noontime meal. I had allowed my elbows to inadvertently touch the table as I sought to devour the tempting delights before me like any hungry young boy. Such lapses in good behavior were not acceptable to Mother. She wanted to impress her debutante friends with her darling, presentable son, and it was her responsibility to ensure his compliance. Our goals, it seemed, were not congruous. She kept repeating that it was essential for boys to have good manners. Each thick book was tucked between my side and my elbow. No part of my body was allowed to come in contact with the table. Those books could have easily weighed five pounds. My older brother Heinz Robert a gangly twelve-year-old with the mind of a college professor, looked straight ahead and chewed slowly, not uttering a word. Next to him at the head of the table, our father Ernst the owner of a thriving wholesale shoe business, recounted the daily occurrences at his workplace, speaking to no one in particular, trying so hard to convince himself that everything was okay. "I am not so worried about the Nazi's as some of you are. I have no political affiliation. I'll just run my business and this will pass," he said. His white shirt was flawlessly pressed and his manicured hands waved with conviction. I wasn't worried about his damned business. I had far more pressing matters on my juvenile mind. Increasingly, I had come to detest mealtime, and I would rather risk being caught late at night raiding the icebox with a guaranteed beating than endure the humiliation and pain of what to many others was the best time of the day when other "normal" families join together in fellowship, eating, while sharing their lives. Feeling short-changed, I often thought of how much we really had to share living this affluent life in a beautiful, cosmopolitan European city. I didn't cry during the meal, instead storing the emotion inside for later. I just formed an invisible wall around myself. I would show Mother that her cruel exercises were well within my limits of endurance. My resolve caused the muscles in my arms to stiffen all the more tightly. I always imagined that I could flatten the books if I chose. Instead of the expected grimace that one might assume would be on my face, Mother would see a slight smirk and I knew it would cause her to seethe in anger. It seemed to me that her mission in life was to make my life miserable. Therefore, my mission, in ever increasing ways, was to circumvent her authority. My beloved grandmother felt the tension in the air and her eyes looked sadly toward the window, my special place. It was the same one where she saw me standing everyday, dreaming of a world where regulations and punishments would be replaced with tenderness and love. I sometimes could detect a small almost indistinguishable tear making its way down her cheek, and I knew we both shared the same disdain for this hopeless existence. We were, unfortunately, equally impotent; but we both had unlimited resolve. My young life was in chaos internally while the world outside was coming apart at the seams.

Thank God for my brother Heinz Robert. Even though he was only a child himself, he gave me so much support in those days. That night he stopped by my bed with some tasty pastries that Grandmother had bought at the bakery that day. We were both covered with crumbs as we snickered about the look on Mother's face during lunch. "We won't tell her that the dog sits between your legs during mealtime and shares the same repast as his master. That clean plate would not be so clean if the dog's portion were still on it," said Heinz Robert as he covered his mouth with his hand to muffle the laughter. He later tucked me between the flannel sheets of the soft feather bed, and mussed my thick, blond hair with his gentle hand. My eyes were so heavy; and as I drifted into the mistiness of sleep that historic night, I heard Heinz Robert's soft voice. "The world is ours to conquer, Otto. Nothing will stop us as long as we stick together. Good night, my dear, sweet brother."

"Good night, Heinz Robert." I didn't know at the time how prophetic his words would be. We certainly did need each other and we could conquer the cruelest of worlds, but only if we did stick together and if I could find a world outside my window where real love existed. I guess I first needed to find out what parental love meant. I sensed that it must somehow involve turmoil because my life seemed so fraught with that. My world was a daily routine of rules and restrictions imposed by my domineering mother and enforced by my subdued father. I was taught the appropriate way to bow when introduced to gentlemen and a proper way to kiss a lady's hand. I even had to kiss my own mother's hand when she came home from shopping. Every birthday and holiday, Heinz Robert and I had to learn and recite a poem for the occasion. If I broke a little rule, my favorite toy was taken away and I wasn't allowed to go outside and play with my friends. If I made my mother angry, I was forced to sit in a corner until my father came home from work; then he would often beat me. I can remember watching in horror as my brother was physically punished because he was having trouble forming a figure eight with his pencil. Many times, when I was playing board games with my friends, my mother would help them win. This was to teach me that I must be a good loser. I learned that lesson every day of my life. My early memories of school were also bitter ones. We had to stand up when an adult entered the room. I also remember trying to write with my left hand, which was not tolerated. When the teacher saw me doing this, he would smack my

hand with a ruler. As each day passed, I understood that all of my daily activities at school and at home would continue to mold me into a showpiece of formality, satisfying my mother's infatuation with the royal family and monarchism. Daily, I began to realize that I played an important role in my mother's fantasy world, where beautiful people dressed impeccably and behaved sterlingly. Touching was minimal and life, while comfortable, was sterile.

After The Anschluss my stress level heightened. The political events increased the personal pressure I felt at home. There wasn't a whole lot to be happy about in those days. So when the story appeared in the paper about the Joe Louis vs. Max Schmeling fight at Yankee Stadium in the United States on June 22, 1938, the Jewish population was ecstatic. Joe Louis knocked out Schmeling in 124 seconds. The defeated Schmeling came home on an ocean liner and had to be carried off the boat on a stretcher. That fight was a disappointment to Hitler because the Nazi's touted Schmeling as a model of the super Aryan. This was one bright spot in a tumultuous year that was turning out to be devastating for my family, in particular, and for European Jews in general.

Eric Kolb was a boyhood friend of my father. He was tall with blue eyes and blond hair. Neither my father nor Eric fit the Nazi propaganda posted in every public place describing Jewish men as weak and unattractive. This placed both men in physical danger when venturing out onto the streets. Eric was a brave man and would often take my brother and me on long walks. I admired this handsome, gentle man. Unfortunately, one day he received a letter from the Gestapo ordering him to report to their headquarters immediately. He ignored the letter. I remember my father asking him in disbelief how he could disregard their demands. He replied, "What they will do to me if I turn myself in will be worse than the punishment I will receive for ignoring their orders." Miraculously, his resourcefulness allowed him to escape with his family to America, inspiring many of his friends to do the same.

The SS was placed in charge of Jewish affairs in Austria with Adolph Eichman establishing an office for Jewish immigration in Vienna. Hitler had established the Mauthausen Concentration camp near Linz. The Nazis prohibited Aryan front ownership of Jewish businesses. We were forced to register our personal wealth and property. Jews were prohibited from trading and from providing a variety of specified commercial services. All Jews over the age of fifteen had to apply for identity cards to be shown on demand to any police officers. Jewish doctors could no longer practice medicine. After the Nazis destroyed the synagogue in Nuremberg, Jewish women were required to add "Sarah" and men required to add "Israel" to their names on all legal documents. Then the Jews were prohibited from all legal practices. A law was then passed that every Jewish passport had to be stamped with a large red "J." The speed at which these methodical attacks were implemented was staggering.

I kept going to the window every day as I had always done and saw people's facial expressions change from happy, to sad... to empty. Those transitions were not unlike my own. I believe that the situation outside my home caused my mother to feel out of control. This sense of loss of power seemed to accelerate her need to manipulate even the slightest details of her children's lives. Even our grooming and bathing became exercises in meticulous regimens. The part in my hair, the way my shirttail was tucked in, and the way my shoes were tied consumed my waking hours instead of carefree playtime.

I watched Heinz Robert work for days designing and building a machine from a play set that resembled a modern-day erector set. When it was completed, he and I would go into our room and operate it, laughing loudly and enjoying ourselves. One day, apparently Mother felt that we hadn't spent as much time as we should on the matters she deemed important. She greeted Father at the door that afternoon and told him that something had to be done about our behavior. He knew she would not be affectionate toward him until he fulfilled her wishes. He stormed into our bedroom, grabbed the model, and threw it to the floor. It crashed into small pieces. Heinz Robert and I did not cry until Father left. My stomach hurt constantly throughout the summer.

On a cool day in November, toward nightfall, I observed a group of people gathering in the street below. They were waving their arms about frantically and talking loudly, nodding their heads in consent. The mobs consisted of Nazi party members, such as SS men in their menacing black uniforms; SA men in their brown shirts; Hitler Youths, adolescents completely brainwashed by the Nazi propaganda machine; and what shockingly seemed to be ordinary people who had been transformed into Nazi sympathizers. These were the same people that we used to meet and greet on the street everyday. Now the humanity within them was dying. As darkness fell on the city, mobs started to systematically destroy synagogues and Jewish-owned properties. I heard my father telling Mother that Jewish citizens were found on the street beaten, some actually murdered in cold blood, left on display as if they were hunting trophies. The next morning the streets were littered with broken glass and burned-out buildings. This night, which became known as "Kristallnacht," was the first of many nights of mayhem and destruction that occurred on the streets of my beloved city. I later found out that this terrible event was precipitated by the assassination of Ernst von Rath, the third secretary in the German Embassy in Paris. He was shot by Herschel Grynszpan, the seventeen-year-old son of one of the deported Polish Jews. Rath died on November 9, opening the floodgates of an accelerated hatred and violence toward Jews. After the assassination, Kristallnacht occurred annually as if it were a national holiday. I thanked God that my windowpane, my precious glass, and outlet to the world, had remained intact and wasn't shattered.

A few weeks later, my mother seeking normalcy said to me, "Let's go to Gerstner's," a famous bakery and coffee shop. We both loved it there. As we sat enjoying our selec-

tion of delicious pastries, I looked up and in the doorway of the restaurant stood SS men. One of them hollered across the room, "Juden Herauss" which means "all Jews must leave." As all Jewish people scurried out of the restaurant, I was temporarily separated from my mother. It was a scary experience for a boy my age. Mother finally found me standing in the street crying and we hurried home.

I could hardly believe that prior to The Anschluss less than a year before, I was the son of a successful local businessman. My father even received the prestigious "Businessman of the Year" award for the city of Vienna. My family had cars with chauffeurs, nurses, maids, tutors, and house servants. There were wonderful times when we would summer in the country on expensive vacations with my parents who lived like aristocracy. I can't recall when it began, or if it was sudden, or if it came in small incremental ways, but my mother was transformed into the most powerful force in our household. We watched the manipulation and control of my previously strong father into total passivity. I began to exert my own personal power by hearing only what I chose to hear.

There were some fond memories. In the early days, the colorful, animated chauffeur Adolph would take us to and from school. On the weekend, we would be driven to the Vienna woods or to the world-renowned zoo. Adolph was a former race car driver and regretted not staying with that occupation. On numerous occasions I was allowed to sit in the front seat next to him, and if an unsuspecting car passed us I would yell, "Adolph, get him." He would pretend he was a race car driver again and step on the accelerator overtaking the car within seconds. I would squeal with delight and excitement and Adolph would wink at me approvingly.

Everything that I tasted, smelled, touched, and saw was Viennese. Being Austrian was a source of pride and helped to shape my identity. I could not wait to grow up and associate daily with people like Adolph, carefree, happy people who laughed often and seldom spoke crossly to each other.

Though I often felt disconnected from my parents, I thought my position as a citizen of Austria was a constant in my life. The opulent surroundings and routine Austrian life seemed so permanent. For me, however, that only was to mean seven years.

The annexation and the events it precipitated changed my view of everything. One day, two Gestapo agents in civilian clothes accompanied by uniformed SS men walked into my father's business and asked for the front door and automobile keys, the combination to the safe, and told my father to leave the premises. My dejected father walked slowly home grieving silently over the loss of his cherished business.

A few days later my proud Mother was accosted on the street by a group of SA men and forced to clean the pavement with her expensive coat, a birthday gift from my father. This experience so traumatized her that she became physically ill and stayed in bed for a week. I would gladly have accepted her old disciplines rather than see her pale, lifeless form in that oversized bed. Soon, all of our luxuries disappeared and our family was forced to focus on survival. Such items as a small carton of sugar or a few ounces of meat were the new reasons for celebration. My father began to realize the only safety was for him and his family to leave Austria. Somehow I believed that he thought if he didn't get my mother out soon, she would simply wither away and die. I sensed that I would leave my home shortly and would often whisper good-byes as I looked out my window. One day as I peeked around the corner, I saw my father staring out my window and he was sobbing. I moved closer and I could hear him whispering over and over again, "Please go away, just please go away."

Then the most vivid and explosive episode started one day as, again, I was staring through the gaps in the curtains. I had seen men in menacing black uniforms approaching our building, walking briskly, and there was a knock at our door. I peeked from my room and saw my grandmother and moth-

er opening the door revealing two huge SS men. Upon closer view, I saw their holstered pistols and shiny boots. I became so frightened that my stomach tightened and I screeched in pain. Then I ran to my grandmother for protection. The men ignored me, instead demanding money from my mother. Like all wives of that day, she told them that her husband handled all of the finances of the household. They growled, "We will wait." The following hours were torturous and seemed like an eternity to me. We all sat on the sofa facing the black-suited monsters. Their faces were expressionless and their eyes were dark and piercing. I began squirming after the first hour and asked Grandmother if I could take my seat by the window. She asked the men and one waved me in that direction with his large gloved hand. I could barely swallow and the overwhelming fear caused my small hands to tremble. I saw my father approaching and pressed my pale face to the window, wishing I could scream. My father didn't notice me and walked briskly to the entrance. He entered the room and the men repeated their harsh demands. He had no choice but to comply. They were not satisfied with the amount he gave them and they dragged my father out the door. He was silent, holding on to his last ounce of dignity in front of his family. I ran to the window and watched them shove him into an awaiting car. I sat by the window and watched the street below as the car sped away. When you have no control, you must rely on patience to be your friend. I realized that the resolve I had developed to not give in to my mother's disciplinary tactics was proving useful in dealing with this newfound, potentially deadly enemy. Mother paced the floor, her heels clicking noisily, and then like the proverbial light bulb coming on, it occurred to her that she had been given a phone number of a business associate of my father's a month before. She dialed the number and told the person answering the phone the whole story. He said he would do what he could this time but to please not ever call that number again. The next morning my father came home, bloody and beaten with large welts on his back and with an indescribable look of fear in his eyes. He could not look at us directly without turning away and I knew irreparable damage was done. For the remainder of his life, he was traumatized by this event. Whenever the Holocaust was discussed, he would have nightmares and would wake up drenched in sweat, screaming. Any knock at the door caused him to shake uncontrollably. This tall, erect man whose strength was wrapped up in the ability to provide for his family learned how fragile the circumstances of life really are and his shoulders stooped. He would never forget his encounter with the devil and neither could I. I no longer feared my father; I felt sympathy for him.

Somewhere in Berlin, the Nazi leadership was smoking cigars and drinking fine brandy, devising plans to control the destiny of countless families including my own. I observed, first hand, just how far-reaching their tentacles were. One day, I overheard my parents and grandmother whispering about a horrible incident that had occurred in our building. Apparently, three SS had men had entered the apartment of the family living on the top floor. The family either could not or would not comply with their demands. The Nazis told the parents that they would throw one of their two children out the window. They saw the terror increase and it inspired them as they forced the frightened mother to choose one of her children to die. The mother became hysterical and reluctantly made a choice. The SS men threw the child not chosen by the mother out of the window. The mother was a young woman whose facial features became drawn and whose hair turned completely gray overnight becoming a shell of a person. After hearing the story, I ran to my window to escape the horror and tried to imagine happy children playing on the street.

As time went on, my mother became depressed and sometimes acted strangely. Her physical appearance changed and she seemed to be shrinking in size every day. Her eyes were sad with dark circles and her voice had lowered several octaves. The woman who was so full of energy was now, at less than forty years of age, lifeless and devoid of spirit. She did not find it in herself nor did she have the desire to ask my father to inflict punishment upon us. She had resigned herself to the ultimate form of control. She wanted to die and she felt it was her obligation, I suppose, to take her children with her. She would often come to me and say, "Let's put our heads in the oven or fill the bathtub with water and drown ourselves." When these events occurred, I became reclusive and ran away to my favorite place, the window, to pretend that it never happened. These suicidal discussions were the most defining moments of my childhood. I often wondered if learning how to die properly was a part of the etiquette that my mother so adamantly insisted that I acquire. I played a new game called "Wonderland," pretending that my window was as magical as Alice's looking glass, and I could travel to a happy place whenever I chose. At the same time Father was risking his life on the streets of Vienna, trying to sustain his family, not knowing of the equally dangerous situation at home. At least, I prayed that he did not!

I opened my eyes and I was glad to be that sixty-eight-year-old man in a hotel room and not the boy, Otto. I looked out the window again. Everything was as it should be. The world was still there. Life was going on. For the second time today, I felt free and relieved. I was in control of my own life.

* * *

Karla had been watching Peter through her window all day. Even when he wasn't speaking she knew what he was thinking. It made her very sad. Between sobs, she uttered words that she knew he was unable to hear. "I never would have hurt you, Peter. I loved you. I loved you and I wanted you to be near me. I wish that I could just have said these words to you." For the first time, it was easy to tell the truth. Suddenly she sensed that someone was behind her and she turned with a start. There before her stood a handsome man with soft, caring eyes. "Hello, Karla, I've been waiting for you. I've been waiting for you for a long time. It's good to finally meet you after all this time."

"Who are you?" she asked suspiciously.

"My name is Abraham. Abraham Kook. On earth, I was the chief rabbi of Palestine and I have been chosen to be your guide. I was misunderstood when I lived on earth, too, Karla. I would say, to some degree, everyone is misunderstood, Karla; but it does sadden us when those who are closest to us misunderstand us the most, doesn't it?"

Karla shook her head affirmatively. "Yes, it does, Abraham. It truly does..."

"Yes, Karla," he replied consolingly.

"I know that I have died, but I have been afraid to ask where I am."

"Do not be frightened, Karla. Here, take my hand and let's go for a little walk together." He lifted her up away from the window.

"I wish to see Otto," she begged.

"Ahh, we will come back in a few minutes. Come with me now," Abraham summoned. Karla stepped to his side. He held his arm in hers and they began walking. She had no idea where they were or where they were going, but she instinctively trusted this man.

"Are we going to meet God, Abraham?" asked Karla.

Abraham stopped for a moment and turned to look at her. He smiled and said, "Everything that has life in it, Karla, everything that exists is the body of God. So, yes, we are. We are going to meet God."

Suddenly, they were walking along a tree-lined path. Everything was a vibrant green. As they rounded a small turn in the path, there sat a man upon a rock. "Hello, Ezekiel."

"Hello, Abraham."

"I would like for you to meet my friend, Karla, Ezekiel. She has just arrived."

"Karla, it is so good to see you. I have a box for you," said Ezekiel.

"For me?" Karla asked. She became excited, *"Is it a gift?"* She had always loved receiving gifts.

"Oh, it is a very special gift. It is a gift for you to give to Peter," stated Ezekiel.

"Oh, that would be wonderful. I've felt so helpless since I got here. I feel strong, but yet so helpless."

"Karla, remember," Abraham said patting her on the shoulder, *"you have all the time in the universe. Be patient."*

Karla was beginning to relax. *"It is not a strong suit of mine, but I will try."*

Meanwhile, Ezekiel had walked behind the rock and had retrieved a beautiful, ornate, black box with gold inlays. Across the top was written the word, Kabbalah. *"But what does this mean, this word?"* asked Karla.

Abraham and Ezekiel looked at each other then Abraham spoke, *"Let's just say it's an ancient Hebrew word which means 'that which has been received.' But for those who are receptive, it also could mean 'that which you are receiving.' And Karla, it may take you by surprise."* With that, Ezekiel and Abraham were suddenly gone and Karla found herself alone in the middle of the room, looking at Peter who was standing at the window. She looked down at the box and slowly opened it.

CHAPTER II

"Things do not get better by being left alone."
Winston Churchill

I was startled by the sudden sound of Bonnie's voice. "Come to bed, Otto," she said sweetly. She used my boyhood name and it was like rewriting the agony of that time with softness and tenderness. As I nestled next to her, she put her arms around my neck, "Your muscles are so stiff and tight, you've got to relax." She massaged my neck ever so slowly and I began to release the tension in my body and my mind; I could feel sleep coming on. As I drifted into that quasi-world of surreal dream images, I could see the cemetery where we were earlier today. It was almost like some cruel joke, a family reunion, a gathering where death had brought us all together. Death, it seemed, was that family member who visited us infrequently, but who always managed to get everybody together for a brief, though rarely comfortable, visit. I wanted dreamless sleep. Please! But it was not to be… I remember suddenly looking around, and everyone was there except for my grandmother. Then, I could hear her voice. She was calling me to come and I ran toward the sound of her voice. I found myself in the middle of a familiar looking cemetery in what I knew was Vienna. I was back in the late 1930s again and I played as if I belonged here. Then I remembered that it was the only place I could play and that made me sad. Jewish children couldn't play in the street anymore for it was far too dangerous. The Jewish cemetery, a place normally associated with death, was where I could be a little boy again and feel totally alive.

After I was exhausted, I went home from the cemetery and found that a family meeting was being held. Everyone

17

looked so serious sitting around the dining room table talking softly. They were considering the various options available to us. Finally, we narrowed our choices down to only two possibilities of escaping alive. My father, assuming the position of leadership, arose and spoke, "We have only two alternatives that are viable to us. We can send Heinz Robert and Peter to England or Palestine, or we can all seek to emigrate to America." I don't know how the decision was reached, but the choice was made that we would all get out together or none of us at all. This disjointed group of genetically attached individuals suddenly looked like a family.

The most remarkable chain of events followed. Somehow my resourceful father was able to secure an American phone book from Chicago and he looked up the name "Abeles." He found two families by that name living there. They were Jerome and Jean Abeles and Theodore and Leah Abeles. My father wrote both families letters describing our desperate situation and our eventual fate if we could not leave the country very soon. To our surprise, both families were sympathetic and agreed to help. I often looked out my window and imagined warm faces in a distant land thinking kind thoughts about me. Fortunately, Jerome Abeles was financially qualified to legally sponsor our family and wrote this beautiful letter to the American Consulate in Vienna.

July 12, 1939
Honorable, American Consul
American Consulate
Vienna, Germany

Dear Sir:

I recently received a letter from Ernst Abeles asking
that I supply you additional information to support
his entry into this country. This is enclosed herewith.
In March of 1939 I submitted to your office an affi-

davit of support in behalf of Ernst Abeles and his family of Vienna. It is my understanding that you are in need of additional information, and this letter is being written in answer to this request.

It is true that it is doubtful whether or not any blood relationship exists between Ernst Abeles and myself, but nevertheless, I am anxious to help him because I believe that I am morally obligated to assist him.

The fact that Ernst Abeles and his family have been deprived of the right to live, through no fault of their own, so completely distresses me that I wish to do everything in my power to assist them in getting into this country and to take care of them after their arrival.

As previously stated in our affidavits, both Theodore Abeles of 3313 West Madison Street in the City of Chicago and myself have guaranteed that Ernst Abeles and his family will at no time ever be allowed to become public charges. Ernst Abeles and his family will reside with Mr. Theodore Abeles and his wife at 3313 West Madison Street in the City of Chicago. Mr. And Mrs. Abeles own their own home, in which they occupy a six room apartment and there is ample room there to accommodate Ernst, Caroline, Heinz and Peter Abeles, and I will gladly provide Ernst with a weekly monetary allowance ample for his needs.

If this does not work out satisfactorily, both my wife and I shall be very happy to have Ernst Abeles and his family reside with us. We have an eight room apartment at 1019 Hyde Park Blvd. in Chicago. Only my wife, our two small children and I reside in this Apartment and there would be ample room to accommodate Ernst Abeles and his family.

As stated in my affidavit, my annual income is sufficient for this task. I am well able to assume responsibility for Ernst Abeles and his family, as outlined in this and previous affidavit.

Respectfully yours,
J. Abeles/FB
Jerome Abeles

Subscribed and sworn to before me on this 12th day of July, 1939.

After my father received a positive response from our sponsors, he formulated a plan for our immigration to America. First, we would wait for the sponsorship papers to get into the proper hands. After they did, we would apply for an exit visa from the Nazi authorities. Then we would apply to the U. S. embassy for entrance visas and we would pack what few belongings we had left.

As my father was formulating this plan, he realized that in order not to be a burden to our sponsors he would have to earn a living as soon as we reached America. But he knew that due to the language barrier and other circumstances, he would not be able to use his work experience to find a job there. He decided that my mother and he would have to learn a trade. Fortunately, the Jewish Community Center was offering courses in various occupations so he chose glove design and manufacturing. My mother went first and learned how to sew gloves by hand. My father then learned how to design the gloves, buy, prepare, and cut the leather. For the first time in many months, I could see hope in their eyes again. The industrious nature of my father amazed me.

After many days of waiting and watching the postman walk past our mailbox, the necessary papers arrived and the immigration procedure began. The first step, obtaining exit permits from the Nazi authorities, was very difficult. After hours of red tape and many personal insults, this was finally accomplished. Then we began the next step of getting the necessary visas from the American embassy. The whole family went to the embassy together, where we were told we had to take physical and mental examinations. The American officials were rude and nasty. This was scary to me. I was not allowed to stay with my mother and had to stand in line naked and embarrassed with the other adult men. For a short time I got separated from my father and brother and I started to cry. It reminded me of the time when we had to leave Gerstner's Coffee Shop. My mother could hear me sobbing so she came to find me. The same woman who suggested we might end our lives together now held me as we were preparing to begin a new life together. This fresh start began with a hug. I wanted to call her Mama. I wanted to forget everything that had happened, but I did neither. I simply relaxed and enjoyed the warmth of her touch. Finally, it was over at the American embassy and we were told to go home and wait for the visas to arrive by mail. A few weeks later our papers arrived. We were now ready to prepare for the journey to America.

The morning after our visas arrived, Grandmother said she was going to take me to the cemetery so I could play. As we walked down the street, Grandmother held my hand tightly. I was frolicking among the gravestones, running and jumping and laughing until I tripped and fell.

As I raised my head, I knew that Otto was gone, the dream over. Now I was again, Peter, and I could smell the fresh dirt of the Long Island cemetery. I looked up and saw a gravestone where the words read, "Ernst Abeles, beloved husband, father and grandfather." I glanced to the side and saw the temporary marker on my mother's grave. Time, in my dream, was bouncing around like my emotions.

I sat up in the hotel bed suddenly wide-awake and I was drenched in sweat. I went to the bathroom where I had several glasses of water. As I drank, my breathing began to return to normal. I walked back, yet again, to that hotel window and looked out. I could see signs of life again. People were moving to and fro, accomplishing their tasks of daily living, alive and free. I closed my eyes again and I focused on the sounds of my beautiful wife's restful breathing as she slept so peacefully. I thought it odd that each life-giving breath we take moves us incrementally farther down the line like a one way train ride to a mysterious destination.

*   *   *

Karla closed the box. She heard another voice and it sounded familiar. "Karla." She turned to see Ernst.

"Ernst, it's been so long. It's been so long." She ran to him. He looked just the same as he did when they vacationed in Monte Carlo. He had on that same suit. "You look fantastic, Ernst."

"And you, Karla, you look beautiful." They held each other. She had not felt the romantic embrace of a man for so very long. She didn't want it to end. After a while, however, he stepped back. "Karla, you know I did what I had to do for my family."

"I've always known that, Ernst," she replied.

"I've heard you telling Peter how frightened you were. Well, you were not half as frightened as I was, Karla. All my life I had been told that a man must take care of his family and protect them. Then when the Nazis came, I felt impotent. I was weak and when they took me to that awful place, after they beat me, I could hear people screaming in other rooms, Karla. I got on my knees and I begged for them to let me go and let me come back home to you. I never felt like a man, a whole man, again. Do you understand?"

"Yes, Ernst, I do. I truly do."

And then Ernst was gone. Karla cried out for him but there was only silence. Then she looked down at the box and the word on top of the box had changed. The letters B-I-N-A-H were there in place of Kabbalah. The silence was broken by the sound of Abraham's voice. "The word means understanding, Karla. The seeds of understanding have been planted. Now, it's up to you."

Karla reopened the box and looked toward the window at Peter again. His eyes were wide open.

CHAPTER III

"The highest wisdom is loving kindness."
The Talmud

I lay in my bed and watched the digital clock advance minute by minute in a predictable cadence. The last time I saw the red numbers it was 1:00AM. Then time moved backward again...

The rhythm of the rail car was making me drowsy and I could already hear my brother sleeping in the seat next to me. The trees rocketed by my moisture-covered window, and I pretended the passing evergreens were anonymous Nazis passing out of my life forever. Good riddance! I glanced across at my parents and though they were silent, their eyes were opened wide. They didn't even seem to blink. Maybe they were afraid to fall asleep and find our miraculous departure was just a dream. The train was crowded with refugees, and there was barely room for our luggage. The silence was more than I could take and I stepped out of the compartment and down the narrow aisle way to the restroom at the rear of the car. There was a long line of people awaiting their turn. I heard a commotion and I remember the gaunt face of a man wrestling his way speedily through the maze of people. I could see two tall men wearing black hats and belted trench coats standing at the front of the car eyeing the crowd suspiciously. The anxious man was suddenly standing beside me and he knelt down to avoid the gaze of the Gestapo agents. When he crouched a coin fell from the pocket of his trousers. I retrieved it and tried to hand it to him. He extended his hand and, rather than take the coin, he allowed his shaking fingers to touch the top of my hand. I shall never forget the look on his face as the expression of terror softened. As quickly as the man appeared, he vanished into the crowd. As I stood again the two Gestapo agents brushed against me then disappeared. I finally made it to the bathroom and returned to my seat. I remember looking at that coin the remainder of the day. Over the next few weeks, it would be a personal reminder of my life in Austria as I rubbed its smooth edges and worn features.

We had left Vienna hurriedly on our way to Rotterdam to depart for the United States. The last few days had been hectic as the time drew nearer for us to leave Austria, never to return again as citizens. America seemed so very far away to me. My mother became more and more depressed about leaving the few valuables she had left that were hidden from the authorities. She declared she would not leave without these items; she was adamant. At first, my father refused to even discuss trying to get these items out illegally. We all knew the consequences if we were caught. As always, my mother's powerful personality prevailed. She had a Svengali-like influence over my father. After making some discreet inquiries, my father made a phone call to a so-called "smuggler" someone had told him about. They agreed to have a secret meeting. Waiting for the meeting was frightening for my father. Had we already been betrayed? Would we be dragged out never to be seen or heard from again? Finally, the dreadful day of the meeting came. There was a loud knock at the door. We were all terrified. I hid behind my grandmother. My father cautiously opened the door and there stood a tall, unshaven, shabbily-dressed man. He was a truck driver who obviously dealt in black market activities on the side. My father told him we wanted to smuggle one suitcase out of the country. The man, speaking in a loud, gruff voice, told my father that the Nazi authorities would not examine the one specially marked suitcase as we made our journey. The man was paid handsomely on the spot. He winked at me and I forced a faint smile. As I watched him jump happily into his old black truck from the windowed perch of our apartment I wondered why my mother would risk all of our lives to take a few valuables she had hidden away? Was it worth the gamble? My mind had told me over and over again that I must be in control of my life or risk losing it.

I gazed out the foggy window of the noisy train. It was a cold and cloudy day. I remembered saying goodbye to all of our friends and family at the station. Looking across at my mother I could see her resemblance to my grandmother, and being reminded of my sweet grandmother, it made me remember how hard it was to say goodbye to her. As she stood on the platform at the railway station, I could see the resolve in her eyes. She was such a strong person. I recall promising her that she would soon be with us again. As nightfall approached, the events of the day took its toll on my young body and I slowly drifted into a deep sleep. As I slept, the train journeyed across the German countryside toward Holland. My slumber was interrupted throughout the night because of the many stops the train was forced to make for "security" inspections. The authorities would come aboard to examine our papers and baggage. We were fortunate they never examined the one specially marked suitcase. After many tense hours, we arrived at the Dutch border, where we all breathed a sigh of relief. For the last time, Nazi authorities boarded the train to examine our papers. The few minutes they took seemed like hours. I can remember looking into the eyes of one of those men in the black uniforms as he looked at me; and for a brief moment, I could see pity in what I formerly viewed as the eyes of a detestable monster. I could sense the presence of a human being. I felt more safe at that moment than I had since The Anschluss began. Later, as the first rays of sunshine signaled the birth of a new day, the spirits of everyone aboard the train seemed to be miraculously lifted. I had never seen Heinz Robert smile so radiantly.

At last, we were out of Germany safely arriving in a free country. A few hours later we arrived in Rotterdam. My father said to us that November, 1939, would be a date we would never forget as we boarded our ocean liner, the S. S. Rotterdam, for our crossing to America. As the huge ship was preparing to weigh anchor, my brother and I were standing at the railing looking at the water in the harbor. He put his arm around me and said, "See, Otto, I told you if we stuck together everything would be all right. You stick with me and we'll conquer the world."

Moments later Heinz Robert jumped up and down and pointed at some dark gray objects floating in the water. A well-dressed ship's attendant came over to see what the commotion was all about. He immediately called one of his superiors and they determined that the objects were enemy mines. Apparently, we were not as safe as we thought. Somehow in spite of the mines, we were fortunate enough to make it out to sea and the long voyage began.

My smiling father came to the deck to retrieve us and we went to our stateroom. My brother and I were shocked to find that we were assigned to first class since we had no money. It was a beautiful room, very large and well appointed. My mother was convinced that we were given first class because of our previous standing in Vienna. (My brother would later tell me it was because our name was Abeles and the rooms were assigned alphabetically.) Regardless, it felt like old times again. We relaxed and chatted as vacationers would of trivial and unimportant matters, as if the last few years were temporarily erased. Later, when we were called to dinner I recall looking at the menu*:

Parisian Salad
Consomme Pate d'Italie
Boiled Mackerel Parsley sauce
Roast Topsirloin of Beef with Gravy
Oysterplants in Cream   Steamed Rice
Boiled Potatoes
Lettuce Salad   French dressing
Ice cream/Moscovite Cake
Coffee

Hmmm, I can still remember the smell of that delicious food, and my mother seemed to have temporarily forgotten the lectures on manners.

---

*Author's note: I recovered the menu from my mother's belongings and felt that it would interest the reader

I was startled from my dream-like state by the sound of Bonnie's voice saying "Otto, honey, we have to get up now if we are going to have breakfast before we catch our flight back to Washington. I let you sleep late. You seemed so restless last night."

"Oh, Bonnie, you don't know the half of it. Boy, I am starving. Let's get breakfast and then head to the airport." I took a shower and dressed quickly then we went down to the café in the hotel. The thought of all that food on the S. S. Rotterdam had left me extremely hungry. The consumption of three eggs, two pancakes, an assortment of fruit, and coffee satisfied my appetite. I read the *New York Times* and worked the crossword puzzle in record time. Later, we took a limousine to the LaGuardia Airport and walked directly to the gate since we had no bags to check. Our plane soon lumbered down that long runway and lifted up slowly. As we banked sharply and the city came into view, outside my window I could see the Statue of Liberty, that gigantic welcome center to the good old U. S. of A. As Ellis Island disappeared beneath me, I shut my eyes and began to think of another time when I saw that welcome center from a different, closer, angle.

* * *

Karla closed her eyes and thought to herself, I remember that welcome center, too, Peter. I, too, was terrified at arriving in America. Then Karla heard a familiar female voice calling her name. "Karla, Karla."

She jumped up and turned, "Mother, is that you?"

"Yes, Karla, it is." She ran and embraced her mother, something she hadn't done very often.

"Mother, we never should have left you in Austria," Karla said broaching a subject that had never been discussed.

"Oh, Karla, you had no choice. You had your children to think about. It was okay."

"I feel so shallow thinking only of my clothes, my jewel-

ry. I put my husband and my children at risk. But for some reason, those things meant so much to me at the time."

"And now, Karla?" her mother asked.

"And now, Mother, they have no value whatsoever."

"That is good," her mother said as she slowly faded away into nothingness.

Karla knew what she must do and she returned to the window and picked up the box. There was a new word now, "Hokhmah." She didn't even bother turning around this time. She knew her new friend was there as she spoke, "And this word, Abraham?"

"This word, Karla, means wisdom. It's the beginning point of all things."

Karla looked through the window and she could see young Otto playing on the deck of the S. S. Rotterdam. She could almost smell the ocean air.

CHAPTER IV

"Life is a series of surprises."
Ralph Waldo Emerson

The first few days of life on the S. S. Rotterdam were very exciting. My brother and I spent much of our time exploring the massive ship from top to bottom. I spent many wonderful hours riding up and down on the ship's elevators. On the fourth day, while playing on the top deck with a ball that a ship's mate had given us, I accidentally bumped into a beautiful young girl and knocked her to the deck. Ingrid introduced herself to me after recovering from her fall. She asked me who was the handsome boy who threw the ball? I told her that it was my brother Heinz Robert, and that we were going to America where he was going to be a famous scientist. She was impressed and Heinz Robert played his role to the hilt. We spent hours walking with Ingrid as our "scientific advisor" taught us about the ocean, the stars, and what to expect in our new home. Often, he would send me on a meaningless errand so that he could spend time alone with Ingrid. I made a friend of my own, as well, and while I can't recall his name, I do remember that we shared a stolen cigarette together in a dark corner beneath a stairway. As we both coughed profusely, we extolled the pleasures of smoking.

The meals continued to be tasty and the first-class accommodations made the ten-day trip seem very short. It was, for the most part, peaceful until the very last day, when the feeling of anticipation was thick in the air. Everyone was excited about the docking, and after seeing the Statue of Liberty, we began to reflect about starting a new life in America. As with all new things, there was a degree of anxiety. As usual, I was looking out the tiny window of our stateroom, and I could see a large American flag with its stars

31

and stripes waving majestically in the distance. Little did I know that at that same time yellow stars were required to be worn by Polish Jews over the age of ten. Shortly thereafter, Adolph Eichmann would take over Section IV of the Gestapo dealing solely with Jewish affairs and evacuation. The Nazis chose a little town in Poland, Oswiecim near Krakow, as the site of the new concentration camp, Auschwitz. At the same time, we stepped off that luxurious boat onto the shore of America with a grand sum of $10.00 to be divided among our entire family.

A little light turbulence awakened me, and for some unknown reason, I reached into my jacket's breast pocket to make sure my wallet was there. There was security in knowing that I had cash and credit cards. I looked over at Bonnie and, sensing my stare, she turned to look at me. Behind her I could see the flight attendant getting ready to mouth the words, "May I get you a drink, Sir?"

"Yes, I would like a glass of white wine. How about you, Bonnie?" I asked hoping she would join me.

"Sure, Otto, that sounds great," she replied. It was early in the day but I felt like a drink would be an appropriate choice at this juncture. The attendant brought us a Chardonnay and we toasted. "To us!" Bonnie exclaimed.

"To us!" I repeated. She told me she loved me and then she lightly touched my arm and asked me the question that I knew she had wanted to ask all morning.

"Are you okay, Otto? I mean, are you really okay?"

I loved this woman and knew I couldn't lie to her so I simply said, "No, Bonnie, I'm not okay, whatever that means. I don't feel remorse and I don't know why. I am not sure exactly what I feel; but I'm not sad, and I don't understand it. People are supposed to feel sad when they lose their mother, aren't they?" My wife started to speak but I held my hand up as if to stop her. "Let's talk later, Bonnie," I said as I turned to look out the window again. I kept my attention on the miniature sights below to prevent further probing conversation. An hour passed and I turned to smile at Bonnie. Her soft blond hair and gentle features warmed the recesses of my troubled heart. She smiled back and I felt reassured that my quietness had not angered her. Thank goodness, we would be landing soon and there would be plenty of time for talk. But for now, my own thoughts seemed to be my closest friend. We landed at Washington National and after picking up our car we drove to our home in Bethesda. I carried the bags in and told Bonnie we would unpack later. I went downstairs, and I sat in my large comfortable chair in front of my big screen television where I lost myself in an Orioles baseball game. Somewhere around the seventh inning I dozed off and it was the fall of 1937 again.

I was in bed, hot with fever and pitifully weak. I was very ill. Heinz Robert had been sent to relatives to stay for four to six weeks since the severity and cause of my disease was unknown. He confided to me in letters that even though he felt badly about my illness, the time he spent away from our parents was a wonderful experience. It was great to be with a loving family away from the harsh discipline of our mother and father I suppose. My illness had started with an inner ear infection and had developed into full blown meningitis. During the day my mother would let me stay in her bedroom. I was touched at this show of compassion. Everyday, Docent Lederer, my pediatrician, would come to examine me and stand before me and shake his head. Three times a week, Professor Poper, the nose and ear specialist would come to examine me. Even at the age of six, I could tell that neither doctor knew much about my illness. I was truly alarmed. My father was unable to show me much affection, but he did manage to bring me a new toy everyday. Unfortunately, there were no hugs. My loneliness was abated because my grandmother came to visit every single day. This was so comforting since I missed my brother very much.

In those days, doctors were given one of three titles, doctor, docent, or professor. Professor was the highest and doctor was the lowest. The size of their fees was a reflection of their title. I remember Professor Poper would arrive in a chauffeur- driven limo always dressed formally in a striped morning coat. I remember that even during my illness I would sneak over to the window, especially on the days Professor Poper was expected to come. I knew that I would wither away if I could not visit my wonderland.

Docent Lederer was a very famous pediatrician. When Jewish doctors were no longer allowed to practice medicine, he became depressed much like the rest of us. His escape from the Nazis became possible when the King of Baghdad sent for him to care for his children. The story goes that he committed suicide after only a few months. He left a note that he loved Vienna too much. It is a myth that everyone was excited about coming to America. No one wants to leave their home.

After many weeks, my illness subsided unexpectedly. There was no explanation from any of the medical practitioners for my sudden recovery. My mother claimed I recovered due to her prayers to her "special God." I often wished that she would share this God with me. I needed a powerful friend to sustain me and keep me company when I felt alone. As soon as I recuperated from my illness, I gained enough strength to return to school. I suspected my fellow students would think I was a ghost. When I looked at myself in the mirror, that's what I saw.

I awoke and it was one of those rare times when I could actually remember my dream. I whispered thank you to my mother. For the first time, it seemed possible to me that her prayers had actually saved me; and I thanked her God (and now my God) that she cared that much. For indeed, it may have been her prayers that saved my life. This is the same life that my mother later seemed so willing to take. No small wonder I was so completely confused.

I bounded up the stairways, grabbed my travel bag, and opened it. I had to open the box that my niece and I had packed when we went through my mother's belongings at her apartment. I grabbed the box, took it downstairs, opened it and rummaged through the pictures. I took out the one of my mother as a vibrant, twenty-seven-year-old bride of Ernst Abeles, smiling with her whole life before her. This was the woman who had prayed for me. I was beginning to feel something and it was bittersweet, but I liked it and I knew that I must dig deeper. I carried the picture around the house with me the remainder of the evening. I looked at it every fifteen minutes or so thinking what she must have been like. What would it have been like to have been her friend and not her son, to know her dreams and aspirations?

I remember looking over while graveside at the two women who had cared for her, one for over thirty years, Regina Kinas. She was softly sobbing, her handkerchief damp with tears. She loved my mother, yet the last few years dealing with her had become burdensome. I could relate because sometimes when Bonnie and I went out for dinner, friends and I would joke about how difficult our elderly parents had become. However, I had a picture before me of a young, vivacious woman with dreams just like mine when I was her age instead of a ninety-eight-year-old woman whose son became physically ill at the thought of having to be in her presence. The same son who, when he visited her, would ask his taxi driver to wait for him because he wanted to be able to leave quickly if the situation became intolerable. I could smell her musty, dark apartment as I thought about my visits. We would begin with small talk and then take our positions in her sparsely furnished living room. I made it a point to never have to sit across from her and have to look her in the eyes. Eye contact somehow meant intimacy and those visits were anything but intimate. The passing of time would come to a halt. I always found myself sitting there wondering what this woman expected of me, how could I possibly give her any kind of pleasure? Often she would instigate an altercation and I suppose she wanted me to react like my father, cowering in her presence and conceding to her, but I could not. I would become livid, shout at her, then find myself racing to

*the awaiting cab. It was like an episode of "The Twilight Zone"
where the same nightmarish event keeps recurring, never ending.
"I call the shots now, Mother. It's my choice when I will come and
when I will go." I've thought about the power that I possessed, the
power I thought I had always wanted. Now I think about how dis-
concerting it must have been for the taxi driver who had to retrieve
me after my visits, a shuttering, angry man whispering to himself
and having a hard time regaining his composure as the car put
miles between mother and son.*

Bonnie and I had a quiet dinner at home that night. Our
conversation was about our children and grandchildren; and
after I kissed her lightly on the forehead, I went down to my
study. The only light on downstairs was a small desk lamp
where I sat and stared at the picture once again. My mother's
lips on the photograph seemed to move. I squinted my eyes in
disbelief. Now I was sure that I was going insane. Then her
image spoke with the same voice I remembered from childhood. However, it was not harsh, not condescending, and not
hateful. Was this truly my mother? It was not telling me to
mind my manners or to kill myself. It was not speaking to me
in a stern, scolding tone, but was saying softly, "Forgive me,
forgive me, forgive me." I found myself speaking to the photograph as if it were a real person.

"I cannot forgive you. How could I? How could I possibly
even consider it?"

Then the voice said, "You will surely die from your
hatred."

And I said, almost mockingly, "Then life is about forgiveness. I suppose I'm to forgive you for everything."

The voice simply said, "Yes."

"Great," I said. "Coming from you. So you die and then you
think you can talk to me. You die and you think you can control
me from the grave. What unmitigated gall. You speak of forgiveness!" I was hyperventilating, I suppose, because I felt like I was
smothering, then tears burst from my tightly closed eyes.

"Who else but me, my son, would need it more?" At that

moment, as quickly as a flash of lightning, I understood that I had no choice but to forgive her because I wanted to live. I did not want to be eaten up with this hatred...this guilt. I needed to live not only for myself, but also for my family. For the first time that I could remember, I obeyed my Mother without question. My unwavering resolve was gone. I opened my eyes and they began to burn so I closed them again then I could hear the voices of others clamoring for my attention, followed by a disturbing silence. From the depths of that quietness I heard the most comforting voice of my life as God asked me gently, "Do you forgive me?"

"Yes," I nodded in affirmation without uttering a sound. "I forgive you for not hearing me when I spoke to you before." The voice faded away into a new peaceful silence. I felt a swell of emotion within me and then I screamed out that I forgave this whole world for inflicting pain upon me. As my eyes returned to the photograph, I knew that included my poor, misunderstood mother. I forgave myself, and that lifelong cloud of guilt that had encircled me vaporized harmlessly into the air. Like young Otto so many years before who stepped off that boat to begin a new life, I vowed to begin my new life. I would have nothing to prove to anyone. I could have value without listing my assets or my stock portfolio. I smiled to myself and arose, walking up the stairs toward my bedroom. I stopped to peek out my living room window. I saw a car pull into the driveway of a neighbor's house. A family emerged from the car, laughing as they went to the front door. After the kids went inside, the young couple lingered outside their front door and embraced, engaging in a long passionate kiss. I guess this was a little gift from above saying to me that history doesn't have to repeat itself. Things seemed okay; and later as I lay in the bed next to Bonnie and shut my eyes, I remembered how my grandmother used to tuck me in and kiss me. For the first time in months, I slept through the night without awakening. Life, it seemed, was on the upswing.

* * *

Karla could not believe that she actually got to speak to Peter through that picture. She had always loved that picture of herself. It really reflected her true nature she thought. "Oh, Peter, I'm sorry I had to teach you another hard lesson but forgiveness can sometimes be the most difficult one of all. See how you sleep now, my son."

Abraham spoke again to her, "I'm so pleased to be your guide, Karla. This is so rewarding. I thank you."

"No, Abraham, it is I who must thank you," said Karla.

"And Karla, remember that God once said to Abram, 'Go forth'. There comes a time when you must do it on your own. You will know what to do, Karla. You will know." Then Abraham was gone. Karla turned back, she saw a new word on top of the box, "Hesed." Suddenly, she knew what Abraham meant. She didn't have to ask anyone. It was clear in her mind that the word meant love. Then she rested. When she opened her eyes there was the most radiant light coming through the window that she had ever seen. She looked beyond the light and she could see Peter looking out the window of his home.

CHAPTER V

"You must be the change you wish to
see in the world."
Mahatma Gandhi

I awoke to a beautiful Friday morning and the sound of birds chirping outside my window. Bonnie had arisen early to play tennis with her friends so I prepared myself a healthful breakfast of fruit and cereal. I turned on the television in the kitchen and started watching a gangster movie on the AMC channel. It was one of those black and white, film noir B movies full of clichéd, tough dialogue, and set in New York City. I began thinking of my first reaction to the "Big Apple."

After we had arrived at New York Harbor and following our indoctrination by the Immigration Department, we were greeted by Jewish friends who had arrived earlier in the United States. While they had preceded us, as non-citizens they could not provide us with anything but moral support. Refugees did not pack much financial clout. The air was filled with raw emotion. I recall that everyone was crying except me. I was filled with fascination. As we drove through New York City to an apartment where we would be temporarily housed, I kept asking my father, "Where are the gangsters?" Based on the stories of the "mean streets" of New York City, I expected to see gun battles on every corner.

I had my first encounter with a real live black person. He spoke to me and smiled widely. I smiled back. The honking traffic, the taxicabs, and the sirens of police cars were overwhelming.

We spent a few days there, and it was pleasurable to be surrounded by friendly faces while immersed in this new culture. I did have a frightening experience in the big city that I will never forget. We walked to a neighborhood market with some of the local children to buy some bread. On the way, we saw a group of children playing stickball in the street. While Heinz Robert and the other children continued on to the store, I lagged behind while watching this fascinating, yet peculiar game. Suddenly, I noticed that I was standing alone on the curb of a New York City street unable to speak the language and feeling more alone than I ever had in my life. I remember screaming at the top of my lungs until I heard the familiar voice of Heinz Robert, who handed me a licorice stick. I was instantly pacified and as we returned to our temporary dwelling, I thanked God for the guardian angel who was my brother.

The train ride from New York to Chicago was more enjoyable than my previous train ride in Germany. Someone had left a stack of American magazines in my seat and I spent many glorious hours looking at the photographs of the war in Europe, which now seemed remote and impersonal. I remember seeing that suitcase full of Mother's valuables and breathing a sigh of relief knowing that the American police would not be interested in its contents. My mother's most prized possessions of jewelry, furs, and silver had made the journey to America unscathed. I hoped that Heinz Robert and I had weathered the same journey with as little damage. The Midwest farmlands and industrial areas passed by my window, and my new home was getting closer by the minute.

It was a bone-chilling December day in 1939 when we arrived at Union Station in Chicago, the Windy City. The station was full of people and festively decorated for the holidays. The chill in the air resounded with familiarity as I recalled the brisk winter days strolling along the street in front of our Vienna apartment. However, I would later discover that the Chicago weather was far more brutal, as were the children in my new neighborhood.

Both of the sponsoring Abeles families were at the train station to meet us. Though we have never made a familial connection, I felt a closeness to these strangers who had shown love to a family they had never met. This kind of compassion was foreign to me as I had not felt as loved by my own parents. After all, these strangers had saved our lives. Jerome Abeles had rented a one-bedroom apartment for us on the south side of Chicago at 55th Street.

I was appalled when we walked into the small, modest walk-up flat with bed bugs and leaky plumbing, a far cry from the spacious apartment in Vienna. I was discovering that freedom carried a high price. I had always dreamt of our family being closer together but not because we all slept in the same room. The shock I experienced was far less than that of my aristocratic mother which she displayed quite openly as she perused her new dwelling.

I, of course, immediately ran to the window to explore my New World. After I familiarized myself with the neighborhood as far as I could see, I couldn't help but remember the old apartment. I remembered the huge children's room with its three large windows. This room opened into an ornate dining room paneled with the finest wood and a cord to signal the servants. Double French doors opened into my parents' room. It served as a living area during the day and my parents' bedroom at night. Each one of the bedrooms was 20' x 20'. The dining room and children's room opened into a spacious foyer. Off this foyer was a gigantic kitchen, a modest cook's room with separate facilities, and a large bathroom. Heinz Robert and I loved our room because we had built in shelving to house all of our favorite toys and books. We had no toys now so a lack of shelving was not a real problem. That night I slept unusually well with an occasional siren interrupting my sleep. The many sounds of Chicago were something I could live with easily.

The next morning, my father announced that he was going to enroll us in school. I would have thought he was joking, but Father did not joke very often. He gave Heinz Robert and me a lecture on how important school was as we ate a modest breakfast of hot cereal. My mother dressed me in short black velvet pants that buttoned to a white silk blouse with the ever-present bobby pin to keep my hair out of my eyes. I was quite a sight! As we walked to school, everyone was staring at us, three "greenhorns," walking down the tough neighborhood street. It was an awkward situation as my father tried to make himself understood to the school officials. It was a lengthy ordeal to say the least. After much gesturing, they finally understood him, registered us, and walked us to our designated classrooms. As I watched my father leave, I became anxious. I was on my own, but certainly not in control. A strange country, a new school, and my inability to speak English were stressful enough. And there was more to come. As I watched Heinz Robert disappear into his assigned room, I held my chest up high; and bobby pin and all, walked bravely into my new classroom. Everyone turned to look and I could have melted on the spot. Fortunately, the teacher was very nice to me. I couldn't understand her, but her tone was pleasant. She introduced me to the class, I nodded to everyone, and she took me to my seat. About ten minutes before the final bell of the day was to ring, I realized that I needed to go to the restroom. I hadn't been all day. I had no way to make this known to anyone; so when the bell rang, I dashed out of the room and started frantically looking for a restroom. A janitor saw me dancing around and pointed to the end of the hallway. Unfortunately, the restrooms did not have pictures on the doors so I had no way of knowing which was for boys and which for girls. As I was running up and down the hall for what seemed like an eternity, I finally spotted Heinz Robert. I ran over to him, grabbed him by the arm and told him in German that I had to go to the restroom immediately. As always, he was there for me and showed me the way.

As the days went by, more and more of the older children began to notice how differently I looked and acted even though I tried to remain inconspicuous. I acted strangely because of the language difficulty. Every day at recess and after school they taunted and teased me unmercifully. At recess I hid, and after school I ran home as fast as I could. I eventually solved my problem by making friends with a boy named Danny Coffey. I'm glad he had an affinity for this underdog because he was the toughest boy in school and all of the children were in awe of him. The word went out that Peter Otto was a friend of Danny Coffey's. From that day on, the taunting and teasing stopped. As time went on, I learned to speak English. My confidence increased as my mastery of the language grew. I finally got up the nerve to tell my mother I would not go to school anymore unless she dressed me in American clothes. Lo and behold, I got my first pair of long pants. I was beginning to feel at home in America. My mother's dark conversations of suicide had ceased the day we left Vienna. She had become superficially subservient to my father until our lives returned to some semblance of normalcy. Then the Viennese rituals began again, starting with mealtime punishment and continual condemnation of our acquisition of disgusting working class habits. She would have been horrified to know I participated in belching contests on the playground and had even sneaked into a local cinema with Heinz Robert to watch American westerns.

The phone rang and I emerged from my reflections and answered it. My grandson Corey was excited because his dad had promised to take him to an Orioles baseball game. I recalled how excited I was the first time I went to Wrigley Field to see the Chicago Cubs play. As good as the game was, it paled in comparison to the taste of the hot dogs. Today, at every opportunity I still relish the taste of a Chicago style "red hot" hot dog with all the trimmings.

* * *

Karla was filled with pride at the ingenuity of her son. "That was wise of you, Peter, to align yourself with that strong young man. I tried to teach you that your mind was your most powerful tool. But it is such a shame we were forced to live in poverty.

She heard a voice behind her. "Karla."

"Yes, who is it? Is that you Abraham?"

"No, it is not Abraham. It is me, Micah."

"Micah?"

"Yes, me, Micah the prophet. Remember what I said about our God. I said God will again have compassion upon us and He will hurl all of our sins into the depths of the sea. You and I both know, Karla, that the poverty does not last."
Karla remembered and she picked up the box again and on the top as before was a new word, "Gevurah." She knew it meant power, the power to rise above any situation.

CHAPTER VI

"I'm a great believer in luck, and I find that
the harder I work, the more I have of it."
Thomas Jefferson

I drove to my office in Laurel, Maryland, that afternoon. The traffic was unusually heavy and I found myself very tense. I gripped the steering wheel and even though I had the air conditioner on, I couldn't keep from sweating. During the trip, I started thinking about my first job after arriving in America.

Every industrious boy in Chicago, at some time or another, had a paper route. My brother got his paper route first; and I guess you could say I began as a part-timer since I only helped him on the weekends. He generally pulled a wagon behind him to carry the papers, and toward the end of the day when the wagon was getting empty, I would always jump in back and Heinz Robert would pull me home. On chilly, blustery winter afternoons I would often cry from the cold. Later, I was able to get my own paper route and earn my spending money. This was a source of great pride to me.

Every Saturday our father would demand a dollar from each of us to buy flowers for my mother. This money generally amounted to about one half of our take-home pay. This was not a voluntary contribution.

Heinz Robert soon moved up in the world; it wasn't long until he was working for the Wiesenfield Florist near our neighborhood. Since entering this country, both my father and mother had worked as glove makers. They were meticulous and did their jobs well. My father was an accountant by education but quickly adapted to his new-founded career. We all focused diligently on the source of our livelihoods for the next eighteen months. American capitalism was suiting the Abeles family just fine. Soon my mother returned to her former position of total control. My father felt the constant pressure to improve our lives, and Heinz Robert and I suffered the brunt of our parents' frustrations, both verbally and physically.

I was beginning to really love my neighborhood in Chicago. I loved the vulgar talk of the street-smart, cool boys and it inspired me to develop a toughness. I would often go into my room and practice my newfound persona. But try as I may, I was unable to disguise the loneliness that I felt inside.

The most wonderful day since arriving in the new country occurred when my grandmother was finally able to join us in Chicago. Since 1940, the Nazi terror had increased in Vienna and my grandmother's letters were becoming more fearful. My father worked hard to ensure that my Grandmother would be allowed to leave Vienna safely. Finally in 1941 she got permission. She made her exit through Portugal, and I eagerly awaited her arrival. In June of that year my father took a taxi to Union Station to meet her. I laughed when I thought about that reunion. Strained would be an understatement. My father and grandmother had an unusual relationship. Other than a cursory "hello" and "goodbye," they had always said very little to each other. This may have stemmed from the fact that she may not have approved of him when he started courting my mother. I overheard Mother telling a new American friend that during their courtship my father took her swimming and later spent the afternoon having a picnic lunch. Grandmother, being a very prudish person, was very upset that a single girl would be caught in a swimsuit in front of a man to whom she was not yet married. Judging from photos of my mother, Father was probably more than willing to take the chance. Regardless of the relationship my father had with my grandmother, I was elated when I saw her familiar figure emerge from that taxi and walk up the steps to our apartment building. She hugged Heinz Robert and me then told us how happy she was to see us. I tingled from head to toe. I bowed and when I was upright again, she embraced me and I melted in her softness. Though I somehow couldn't say the words, "I love you," I knew that she sensed it. I prayed that she did. She looked, smelled, and felt just like I remembered her.

Now that we had moved into a larger apartment, we had plenty of room for my grandmother; and we were excited about her taking over cooking responsibilities. My grandmother was a wonderful cook! I remember coming home for lunch and requesting one of my favorite meals, a bacon sandwich. Grandmother was an Orthodox Jew and the odor of fried bacon offended her. However, she would grit her teeth, put a clothespin on her nose, and fry the bacon. I know that she dreaded those times but she really loved me! I'll have to admit, though, it was a funny sight.

On a bright December morning that same year, Heinz Robert and I were listening to the radio together when a news bulletin interrupted our program emotionally describing the Japanese bombing of Pearl Harbor. We ran to tell our father who, had left the room to pour himself a cup of coffee. He called my mother and grandmother and we all listened together. Father stated that this unexpected event would be the deciding factor that would plunge America into the European war. Heinz Robert declared "I will soon have an opportunity to repay that Nazi son of a bitch for taking our home." My mother and grandmother gasped in disbelief at hearing my brother's statement. My Father mockingly scolded him saying, "Now, now, we will not have talk like that in front of the women." I could see that he was actually proud of Heinz Robert. My brother would ultimately end up a soldier in the United States Army and would do his part in bringing some Nazis to justice. At the moment, all I could think about was what it had taken to get our family in one place and I never wanted to be separated from Grandmother again. The newness of us all being together would wear off quickly.

My grandmother and mother had never been very compatible and soon they began to argue often. Most of the fights were a result of my mother's treatment of Heinz Robert and me. At eleven years of age, I was turning into a gangly adolescent with long legs and big feet.

Heinz Robert and I had returned from running errands for Mother. I was carrying a large sack of dry goods, and as I entered the apartment, tripped and lunged forward. When I did, I fell over a small table that splintered into pieces along with a vase containing flowers. Heinz Robert burst into uncontrollable laughter as did my grandmother, who bent over holding her stomach. As I lay on my back with a rose laying across my chest, Heinz Robert said, between guffaws, "May he rest in peace." Mother entered the room to see what the commotion was all about and stood over me. "Hello" I said, embarrassed but also relishing this moment of attention that I was getting.

"Clean up this mess and try not to be so clumsy when you use your own money to replace the table and vase." My grandmother stopped laughing instantly and followed her into the kitchen. While Heinz Robert picked me up from the floor I listened to the ensuing angry exchange in Austrian as an amused spectator, hoping that my grandmother would ultimately bend my mother over her knee and give her a spanking. Unfortunately, loud screaming and arm waving was all that ever occurred.

I began to understand the root cause of my mother's anger when my grandmother blurted out, "God took my good child and left me with you." There was a silence after these words were said. Unfortunately, these words were spoken often. Grandmother was referring to her firstborn son who died when he was a child. When the ever increasing fighting became unbearable to my father, he decided that my grandmother must move out. Actually, I doubt it was his decision. I think my mother instructed him to inform my grandmother of "his" decision. I cried when I looked out the window and saw "Pippin," our nickname for my grandmother, stepping into a waiting taxicab with her small worn bag of clothes. My father had found her a modest room nearby but she almost always visited us on a daily basis. This privilege was based upon her ability to strictly adhere to my mother's guidelines for how Heinz Robert and I were to be treated. I spoke to my mother only when spoken to and in the manner that she expected because I wanted to see my grandmother every day. It was like a gift from God to see her face as she entered the apartment.

By this time, my father's glove business had grown so rapidly that my parents couldn't keep up with all the orders they were receiving. Sometimes my mother would sew hand-made custom gloves into the wee hours of the morning. I watched their drive and I saw that material things could be acquired in this country through hard work. I liked for them to be busy. They didn't have a lot of time to concentrate on Heinz Robert and myself and our multitudes of imperfections.

I saw two curly little whiskers extending from my chin as I eyed my reflection staring back at me from my bedroom window. Manhood was around the corner, I could just feel it.

Our ever-present friend Jerome Abeles introduced my hard-working father to Robert Rohner who owned a company that sold costume jewelry to retail stores. The two men liked each other immediately. He offered my father a job as a traveling salesman. My father decided that he would make gloves for special customers only and accepted the offer. My father's routine was almost unthinkable then, and would be totally unheard of today. He went on the road carrying five large sample cases and used Greyhound buses as his method of transportation. His Austrian accent was still quite heavy, and in the smaller towns he had trouble communicating with some of the locals. He carried a card in his pocket, and when he found a hotel, he handed over the card that simply read, "Give me a room, please." It was almost beyond belief that the man would be gone for two weeks at a time riding the bus across the Midwest. Astonishingly, it wasn't long before he became the "star" salesman.

I really needed my father at this time of my life. I was lonely and I needed his male guidance to tell me what was going on in my head and with my body. There was no way I could ask my mother or grandmother. But Father was too busy earning a living. I guess it was at that point that I decided that was what men do. They earn a living, work really hard, bring home a lot of money, and they give it to their wives who take care of their children, their trophies. It's a small price to pay to relieve oneself of an emotional responsibility. Unfortunately, I learned that lesson all too well. The lessons that seem to resonate the best are ones that don't require a single exchange of words.

I pulled my car into the parking lot of my office. I walked up the steps, greeted the girls in the front, and made my way down the hallway to my office. I passed my son-in-law Lloyd's office on the way. "Hi, Pete, it's good to have you back."

"Hi, Lloyd, it's good to be back."

He asked, "Are you okay?"

"Yeah, I have just been thinking about a lot of things the last few days." I answered. "How are things going here?"

"Oh, fine," he assured me. I looked at Lloyd and was proud to have him in the family. He runs the business for me understanding that he will eventually own FLOM Corporation. Lloyd's work ethic and vision is reminiscent of myself at his age. The efficient manner in which he runs the business, enables Bonnie and me to spend a good deal of our time in Naples, Florida.

Bonnie and I were attracted to the warm, sunny climate; and often I would sit in a big comfortable chair, strategically placed, so that I could look out the window and stare at the peaceful blue-green waters in the Gulf of Mexico for hours.

I sat down behind my desk to make a few phone calls and I couldn't help thinking about my father.

It was hard to believe that after just six months as a traveling salesman, Mr. Rohner, who was nearing retirement, and my father struck a deal whereby my father would purchase the jewelry business with little cash down and through installment payments would own the business. Jerome Abeles, our mentor in America, was thoroughly impressed with my father's performance. Father's confidence grew daily, and his mastery of the English language was improving rapidly. My mother was able to quit work and though her appetite for shopping wasn't quite the same as it was in Vienna, she was showing a propensity toward her lifestyle of the past. While my father's business career was blossoming, Heinz Robert and I continued to work hard in school. He was a gifted student and all of the teachers at his school realized it. It was becoming tough to live in his shadow. I decided that I could never surpass Heinz Robert's intellect, and would have to find another vehicle to prove myself. Meanwhile, he was drafted in 1944 and in that same year became a U. S. Citizen. He sent us a photograph of himself in uniform and this dashing figure sent me spiraling into another bout of feeling inadequate. I began reading biographies of the "Captains of Industry and Business." I practiced being rich and I would walk to my window and pretend that I was looking out over my holdings. I don't need to be a genius. I can hire them to work for me.

Heinz Robert scored so highly on the Army equivalency test that he was chosen for counterintelligence in September of that year. The entire family was very proud of him.

In December, I got an award for collecting waste paper for the war effort. I guess you could say that began my career in trash which would later become a source of acquiring wealth and an opportunity for me to become an independent businessman controlling my own destiny.

I was fortunate enough to land a job at the Chicago public library earning a whopping $.35 an hour. It was good to be in the big bucks! I bought myself a money clip and always kept at least a dollar in its clasp. "Never be without cash." I would tell friends. While I was spending time at the library reading about my heroes of capitalism, Heinz Robert received his first duty post in Germany in 1945, becoming a bit of a hero himself. He was given the task of interrogating Germans to ascertain if they had affiliations with the Nazi party. His analytical mind lent itself to becoming quite an investigator.

One interesting story occurred when he was questioning a suspected Nazi sympathizer. The man confidently asked my brother if it would be possible for him to locate one, Ernst Abeles of Vienna, Austria. He assured my brother that Mr. Abeles would be able to vouch for him, unaware that he was speaking to Ernst Abeles' son. Heinz Robert recalled the man's name from conversations he had with my father; and this man was in fact, the manager the Nazis appointed to run my father's business after it was taken from him. Heinz Robert never told the man who he was, but later told me that he had the lying scoundrel thrown into prison.

He was instrumental in capturing Axis Sally, famous broadcast propagandist for the Nazi government, German equivalent of Tokyo Rose. I was proud to have Heinz Robert do his part to punish the Nazis for their atrocities committed against my family and Jews throughout Europe.

In 1947, Heinz Robert came home and began his studies at the University of Chicago. I continued my high school studies and our Father continued to manage his flourishing business. Mother's wardrobe was expanding, and the post war boom was beginning.

Heinz Robert had a new girlfriend and I could hardly wait to get home from school the day he brought her to meet Mother. I had been overhearing conversations between my parents and I knew they were not thrilled about my brother's new friend. She was a young, witty girl named Barbara. She was not Jewish and my mother, of course, was not pleased. The minute Heinz Robert and Barbara walked in the door I could feel trouble brewing. They were both dressed in blue jeans and after introductions Mother looked Barbara up and down and said, "Why are you dressed like a dirty little boy?" I really felt sorry for both of them. Barbara was too flabbergasted to reply. My mother seized the opportunity to give a long lecture on how a proper young lady should dress. The entire visit lasted only fifteen minutes. Heinz Robert ignored mother's snubs and told me it was time for both of us to live our own lives. Soon after that, Heinz Robert announced his intention to marry Barbara. My parents objected so adamantly that the two planned to elope. Several weeks later, while my parents were away on a trip, Heinz Robert and Barbara were married by a justice of the peace.

In that same year, our family moved again. We acquired a larger apartment on the affluent north side of Chicago, and my father bought his first automobile, a black, 1949 Chevrolet. I remembered how happy he was when he brought that car home the first day. He snatched all of us and we took a long ride ending at an ice cream parlor. I licked my melting chocolate cone while watching my father wipe the fenders of his new car with his handkerchief. He grinned from ear to ear. I remember my Mother looking at the new ring she had received as her reward for being a good wife.

I spun around in my office chair, got up, and walked over to my window to look out at my car. I probably beamed the same way the day I brought it home.

* * *

Karla smiled and reflected back to that glorious afternoon. "Oh, yes, Peter, your father surely had a beautiful car. He was so proud of that car, and I was so proud of that ring, Peter. It was the nicest gift I had received since we had come to America, and you know how I loved jewelry. And your car, is beautiful, too. But, Peter, it is really not about things that I am concerned. Not like I once was."

Karla heard a new voice. She had come to expect new voices.

"So, who is it?" she said almost mockingly.

"It is me, Isaac. I have a message for you, ancient yet new. Strive to see supernatural light, for I have brought you into a vast ocean. Be careful! Strive to see, yet escape drowning."

Karla lifted the box. The word "Rahamim" was there. She knew it meant compassion. She gazed through the window, and in the distance she could hear a telephone ringing.

CHAPTER VII

*"If you judge people, you have no time
to love them."*
Mother Teresa

The telephone rang interrupting my thoughts about automobiles, past and present. It was my stockbroker with his usual list of hot tips, but my thoughts were concerned with emotional rather than financial matters. I told Sandy, my secretary, to take a message and as I disconnected I hit my "do not disturb" button. I needed silence.

My thoughts returned to my mother and a phone call I had received from her in early May. She called often and would sometimes make up stories regarding her health. Therefore, I wasn't too concerned when she telephoned that day and said that she had to be admitted into the hospital for two days to get some blood transfusions. She had a history of being anemic. She wanted me to come and take her to the hospital. However, I was not in the position to drop everything and fly to New York on such short notice. I felt that her caretakers could do it since I had no reason to believe this was a serious condition. They took her to the hospital and checked her in. I began to get phone calls from her saying that the personnel at the hospital were not treating her well. Eventually, she received two blood transfusions and was released from the hospital the next day.

As I reflected on my mother's illness and the possibility that she might soon die, it occurred to me how much she would need my support. I wondered if I would be able to provide it when the time came.

Then I recalled a day many years ago when I stared out the window of the men's room at my old high school. In a few short hours I would receive my diploma and be considered an adult. As I listened to the speeches at my high school graduation, I realized an important phase of my life was over. As I thought about my freshman year, I knew I was still speaking German at home and English everywhere else. The pressure of starting high school and juggling two languages was too much for me so I began stuttering. This made my life miserable, especially when I had to read aloud in class. One day, while I was standing at my locker, one of the prettiest girls in the whole school named Sarah came up and asked me if I had the English assignment for the next day. I tried to answer her but I was stuttering so badly that the words wouldn't come out. Some boys overheard and began laughing. For the next few weeks, from time to time, I could hear people yell from across the hallway, "P-P-P-Peter, P-P-P-Peter." I was humiliated. I received no support at home from my parents. All they did was tell me to talk the "right way." Heinz Robert and my Grandmother tried to help me as much as possible. But ultimately I knew I would have to help myself. I would go into my room and read stories from the Chicago Tribune over and over again until I repeated the lines flawlessly. Gradually, my stuttering lessened, but the balance of that year I had to deal with my voice changing and the appearance of pimples on my face. I didn't participate in football, basketball and baseball. Instead, I ran around the school track when no one else was there, a solitary figure pushing myself physically, toughening myself mentally, preparing for the day when I would be on my own. I began to make friends, learn the proper way to smoke a cigarette, to appreciate Sinatra, and discovered the joys of high school romance. At home, I just pretended to do everything Mother's way. I would lie in my bed at night, my hands clasped behind my head and convince myself that I had the qualities of a great actor. Who knows, I might even move out to Hollywood one day.

After graduation, I decided to follow in my brother's footsteps and go to the University of Chicago. My father did not approve of this university as he considered it to be a very liberal institution. He used his evaluation of the school as an excuse to refuse to pay my tuition. My high school teachers and friends scoffed, telling me my grades were not good enough to be admitted. I didn't listen, took the entrance exam, and to my surprise was accepted to begin college in the fall. I had no money saved and there was only three months remaining before I would have to pay for the first year's tuition.

I applied for a job driving a taxicab at the Checker Cab Company and was offered a job if I joined the union. At the union hall, I was told the fee was $75.00 to join. My heart sank because I didn't have the money. As I sadly turned away from the counter, I bumped into a short, stocky man who had just come into the office. I started to apologize for bumping him when he said, "What's the matter, kid?" I told him about starting college in the fall and not having the money to join the union so I could get the money to pay my tuition. He took out a huge wad of bills, peeled off $75.00 and handed it to me, stating that he expected me to pay it back when I started working. I took the money; but before I could thank him, he disappeared into one of the offices. I returned to the counter and handed the money to the clerk. She asked me if I knew who had given me the money and I replied that I didn't. She told me it was Joey Glimco, the union president, known for his tough demeanor and powerful friends; and that I had better be sure he got his money back. I grabbed my union card and dashed out of the office. I started driving the next day and by working long hours, seven days a week, I managed to earn enough money to pay my first year's tuition. Of course, I paid Mr. Glimco back first. I attended class all day, drove the cab until about 2:00AM and tried to study before hitting class the next day. I continued to receive no financial help from my parents. This grueling schedule took its toll and after two long hard years I gave up and decided to sign up with "Uncle Sam."

The Korean War had begun, and rather than wait to be drafted, I volunteered for the U. S. Air Force. In January 1951, I left for basic training at Lackland Air Force Base in San

Antonio, Texas. After arriving, I discovered that to the locals with a Texas twang, I was just another Yankee.

I found myself back in the present when Lloyd knocked on my door and said, "Pete, we can handle things around here. Why don't you go on home and take it easy." He was right so I went home since my mind clearly wasn't on business matters. The next couple of days were gloriously ordinary. I decided that a round of golf was definitely in order, so I drove to my country club to participate in the ultimate modern male diversionary tactic. As I completed my tee shot on the tenth hole, my cellular phone rang and I jogged to my golf cart and answered it, breathing heavily. It was Bonnie, stating that Mother's caretaker had phoned saying that she couldn't get in Mother's apartment. Since the phone was off the hook, she couldn't call either. They were in the process of getting the janitor to climb through a window to see what was going on inside. I immediately went home and waited for the next phone call.

As I stared at the receiver, it occurred to me how a crisis places the human brain on automatic pilot. All systems were preparing for a possible assault and the troops, while restless, were in a state of readiness. A far cry, I thought, from my first days of military service.

As I sat in the barber chair watching my hair fall all around me, I realized I was really in the Air Force getting my first GI haircut. What had I done? Had I signed up for four years of military service? In a way, I was relieved because I was finally free of my parents' domination.

The winter of 1951 was one of the coldest on record and I found basic training to be very difficult. The training camp was overcrowded due to the Korean War and blankets were in short supply. Like many other recruits, I came down with pneumonia and spent a few days in the hospital. The remainder of my basic training went by without any problems.

After basics, I was assigned to radar school in Biloxi, Mississippi. That consumed forty-two weeks, eight hours a day, six days a week. Luckily, I was assigned the midnight to 8:00AM, shift, escaping the heat of the day. I settled in to the military routine consisting of school, KP, and drinking beer with my newfound buddies. As time went by, I realized what a sheltered life I had been leading. Drinking bouts, womanizing, gambling, and fighting became a way of life. My "Mr. Hyde" alter ego reared its ugly, fun-loving head. The weeks went by quickly and the formerly pale, skinny kid became a muscular, tan young man full of piss and vinegar. I broke some rules and received the usual punishment—-extra KP.

It was Sunday night and my buddies and I were all scheduled for KP the next morning. We decided to go out and celebrate, staying up all night. It was great. We had dinner and visited all of our favorite hangouts. Then at 3:30AM we headed back to the base. As we neared our home base, I spotted a drive-in restaurant that had a large sign by the front door reading "Closed on Monday." I pointed to the sign and suggested to my friends that we take it and hang it in front of the mess hall, the one where we were scheduled to pull KP that day. We looked at each other and started laughing, grabbed the sign and headed home. At 5:00AM we reported to the mess hall for duty. The mess seargent prepared the morning meal and we got everything ready to serve the troops. At 5:30 we opened the door and sat around with sly grins on our faces, as the other men on KP couldn't understand why nobody was showing up for breakfast. By 6:00AM, the mess seargent was frantically pacing up and down. At 6:30, he received a call from the other two mess halls telling him they were overrun with hungry men. He looked over at my buddies and me, getting very suspicious. He stepped outside and saw the sign. Boy, was he hot! He ripped the sign down and returned to our table. Putting his head directly in my face, he asked, "Abeles, are you responsible for this screw up?" I couldn't help but admit my guilt. My punishment was an extra week of KP, but the fun we had that morning made it worthwhile. One day I was summoned to the company commander's office where he made me stand at attention in front of his desk and sweat for a few minutes before he said a word. I could not imagine what I had done wrong. He shoved a piece of paper into my hands and growled, "Read this." I could not believe what I was reading. It seemed my parents had written a letter complaining that I was not writing home on a regular basis, which was causing them undo concern. The rest of my time in Radar school I had to report to the captain's office once a week and write a letter home. It seemed my parents still had some control over my life. I did, however, feel that I was growing up and gaining self-confidence. After the completion of Radar school, I returned home on furlough to find that nothing had changed.

While at home, my father tried to set a curfew for me at Mother's prompting; and I calmly explained to him that I was twenty-years-old and was no longer under his control. I then stood there and stared at him unblinking. He didn't like my perceived insolence but maybe I gained some respect because he turned away silently. The highlight of my visit home was when my father surprised me the next day by giving me his old car, the '49 Chevrolet. My father always gave me toys instead of affection or even attention. We take what we can get. I threw a couple of cases of Old Style Beer in the trunk and headed south.

I arrived proudly at my first duty post in style, driving my first car. It was amazing to me that no matter where I was stationed or how hard my duties were, I always had this burning desire to work and earn extra money. I guess this came from my childhood days and that first paper route. I always managed to find outside employment throughout my service career. My jobs ranged from setting pins in a bowling alley, to driving a Pepsi Cola truck, and working in a meat packing plant.

January 1955 rolled around quickly. I found myself sitting in the captain's office waiting for my discharge papers and bonus pay. My four-year hitch was over. I was ready to go home and begin my life as a civilian. I even had some money in my itching pockets! I loaded the car, said goodbye to my service buddies, and headed for Chicago.

As I drove home, I had a lot of time to think. I thought about Heinz Robert. He would soon get his Ph.D. from the University of Colorado and had been accepted as post doctoral fellow at Harvard. We had stuck together, but he had a promising career ahead of him as well as a wife. He would not have much time for his little brother to hang around. So, I started thinking about my own future. I had two options. I could go back to school and use the four years of GI Bill that I had coming to me, or I could listen to the urgings of my father and go to work for him. I was drawn back to the family I was so conflicted with. Why? I didn't know, but the trip went by quickly and soon I saw the "Entering Cook County" sign letting me know Chicago was near.

* * *

Karla suddenly dropped the box that she was holding carefully in her delicate hands. It fell to the floor with a crash. She pressed her face to the window and she screamed for Peter. "My son, my son, can you feel my pain, my son?" Her knees buckled and she collapsed. "Pick me up please from this cold, cold floor."

There were no voices this time. She was all alone.

CHAPTER VIII

"Love…is a living reality"
Albert Schweitzer

A few hours later the caretaker called us at our Bethesda home and said they had managed to get inside and found Mother lying on the floor. She had suffered a heart attack but was alive and somewhat coherent. The rescue squad was summoned and she was taken to the hospital. Since Mother lived in New York, the caretaker suggested that I not come for a few hours because there was nothing I could do while she was waiting at the hospital. I delayed a few hours then called the emergency room to see if I could get any information on her condition. I was able to reach the caretaker and she said, "Hold on and I will let you speak to your Mother." When mother picked up the phone, she was coherent but sounded weak. I remember she said to me, "Peter, I am very, very sick and I can't talk anymore." That was the last time I spoke with my mother.

One hour later, Bonnie and I were on the plane to New York. Upon arrival late in the afternoon, we took a taxi directly to the hospital. When we reached the intensive care unit, the caretaker filled us in on her condition then took us to my mother's room. I was shocked at what I saw. She appeared as though she had aged twenty years since I had seen her the last time. Lying in the bed, she looked as if she weighed only ninety pounds. She had a breathing tube inserted in her mouth and had difficulty moving her body. She could not speak but used her eyes to convey her feelings. The caretaker, sensing that we wanted to spend time alone with my mother, left the room so we could sit by her bed. I felt extremely uncomfortable so I proceeded over to the closest window and looked out. Bonnie was talking to Mother and holding her hand while motioning for me to come back over to the bed. As I looked down at my mother, it seemed that she was indicating that she did not want the breathing tube. I remembered that she had a "Living Will" and an addendum to it stating that she did not want to breathe by artificial means. After waiting awhile, I began to feel uneasy again so I wandered out into the hallway to find the doctor in charge. I showed him the Living Will which was in my possession, and questioned him about the breathing apparatus. He informed me that these papers gave me the authority to order the hospital to remove the breathing tube. My first impulse was to have this done immediately, but Bonnie prevailed upon me to wait and do it the next day. We stayed in Mother's room for some time. She seemed upset and was actively moving her hands and eyes. It was a horrible sight. We finally decided to leave, go have dinner, and return the following morning.

Since everything was within walking distance of the hospital, we went to a restaurant and immediately ordered some gin. As we sipped our drinks, we started talking about the situation and how we should proceed. Bonnie suggested that I call my brother and talk it over with him. We finished our dinner and went back to my mother's apartment.

The minute I walked in I realized how much I hated this apartment where she had lived for the past thirty years. The only window there was opened onto a courtyard. The furniture was old and depressing and the apartment was dark. Strewn about the rooms were mementos and pictures. Everything I looked at or touched brought back memories. Bonnie and I sat in the apartment just looking at each other. What a depressing place this was to live. I picked up the phone; and after hesitating for a minute, I started to call my brother. Suddenly, I remembered that this is not the brother I could turn to. This is the brother who is now suffering from Parkinson's Disease to the degree that he sometimes has hallucinations from the drugs that control his trembling. I wondered if I called him and he is sick what would I do? I hung up the phone quickly. I sat and reflected a moment, then dialed Heinz Robert's number and he answered the phone. I thought to myself how glad I was that he seemed lucid. I relayed to him the events of the day, and I told him that my feelings were that we needed to remove the breathing tube. He agreed and then there was a silence. He said, "Pete, I can't talk to you anymore. My hands are shaking so badly that I can't hold the phone. Call me tomorrow." He then hung up. I realized there had been a role reversal. I could no longer depend on him, for the first time in our lives, he was depending on me. Wow! I sat looking at Bonnie, realizing she had overheard the conversation and noticed tears in her eyes. We talked for a while, then went to bed in the dismal, dingy place that my mother called home.

As it was my habit, I awoke early the next morning. I didn't want to wake Bonnie, so I got up quietly and walked over to the window. I couldn't see anything out this window but a dirty courtyard. I got dressed and went outside to get some fresh air. I walked approximately forty-five minutes trying to plan what we would do that day. I had almost decided that I would order the breathing tube removed. Upon returning from my walk, Bonnie was up and dressed. We walked over to the restaurant, had breakfast, and proceeded to the hospital. Upon entering my mother's room, she became agitated. She kept grabbing Bonnie's hand and tugging at it. Even though she shouldn't have any strength, she seemed unusually strong.

I searched out the intern and told him that I had discussed it with my family and we had decided that we wanted the breathing tube removed. I assumed that they would do this immediately. The intern informed me that the doctor who was in charge of her case was the only one who could authorize removal of the tube. He also informed me that at the present time she was not at the hospital, but in her office seeing patients. He said he would call her so I could talk with her. I picked up the phone and told her how I felt and what I wanted to do. She said, "I'm not in the business of killing people. I don't agree with your decision to remove the tube. I'll talk to you when I get to the hospital." We both hung up. I was furious. Bonnie and I spent the remainder of the day in and out of my mother's room. During that time, Bonnie sat by her bed talking to her while I wandered about the room, sometimes standing by the bed looking at her, and other times gazing out the window so that I wouldn't feel so uncomfortable. I hadn't felt this way since Vienna, since the time Mother had told us we must die. Well, she was going to get her wish today many years later. Why in the hell did she have to involve me in these death plans every time.

Finally, the doctor arrived at about four o'clock in the afternoon. Again, she started to lecture me about the consequences of removing the tube. I became very angry. I yelled, "I don't need a lecture. I want the breathing tube out." The doctor became hysterical, started crying and ran down the hall. I stood in the hallway not knowing what I would do next. I felt the walls closing in on me. I needed a window, needed to see out. I was startled by the voice of the intern who came back to tell us that the doctor was trying to compose herself and that she would have a meeting with the interns and the nurses soon. She also wanted us to attend the meeting. Bonnie and I went into the room where we met with three doctors and two nurses. Our doctor rose to her feet and began to speak but I stopped her immediately, saying, "Either you remove the breathing tube or I will get someone else to do it." Then it seemed as if the whole world came to a stop. No one else was in that room but the boy, Otto, and me. He looked up at me with those sad eyes and said, "What if no one else will do it, Peter? Will you do it? Will you take Mother's life like she wanted to take mine?" And as quickly as the world stopped, it began moving again rapidly and spinning. I turned and pushed the door open. Bonnie came running after me, worried that I might suffer a heart attack because I had become so agitated. I paced the floor while she went in and sat with my mother. Nearly sixty years have passed since those fateful days when there was talk of suicide and I had no control. I was forced to make the ultimate human decision of life or death. After what seemed like an eternity, the doctor came out and said that she would authorize the removal of the breathing tube.

We went back to Mother's room for the procedure, but Bonnie decided she didn't want to be there. The doctor who was to remove the tube, two interns, and the doctor who was in charge of the case were there. I stood very closely because I wanted to see the entire process. They removed the tube and amazingly enough, she started breathing on her own. Her facial expression became calmer and she seemed to be more relaxed and comfortable. The doctor said, "We will leave you alone with your mother. Call us when you need us." I sensed that their feeling was she would not survive without the tube. Bonnie came back in the room and we sat next to her bed. I was watching the instruments. Her vital signs were strong and she continued breathing on her own. It was unbelievable. I found myself wishing she had died. It was a horrible thought but there it was. We stayed at the hospital a few more hours during which time my mother remained in stable condition.

When Bonnie and I left the hospital, I said, "I need to go home. I need to sit in my favorite chair. I can't stay here any longer." We packed, caught the next shuttle, and returned to Washington. On the way home, Bonnie and I chatted about the day's events. Suddenly I blurted out to her, "What if she doesn't die? What if she lingers on unable to communicate?" Bonnie touched my arm and said, "Don't think about it for awhile. Try to go to sleep." I reclined the seat, relaxed, and fell asleep. I woke up as the plane was landing in Washington. As we arrived at our gate, I thought of my homecoming from the Air Force years ago.

Coming home was not what I had dreamt about. In fact, it was a real letdown. My mother immediately criticized my clothes and my haircut. My father handed me an itemized bill stating that he had kept up with all the money he had sent me the last four years. "This is what you owe me." I was really hurt. I could not wait to get out of the house to visit my dear grandmother. I told her about life in the service and my disappointing homecoming. She told me to be patient and that she was sure my parents loved me. I don't know how she knew that when I had never felt their love. Maybe they felt a sense of responsibility, but love, never. The next day, we discussed my options, and my father convinced me to come to work for him. I felt an obligation to pay my recently revealed debt. We mapped out a program whereby I would spend a few days in the office then go on the road with one of the more experienced salesmen. My father bought me a new car, pointing out that the car belonged to the company. He expected it to be kept immaculately and I was responsible for all damages.

I learned fast and was soon ready to go on the road by myself.

Prior to going on my first sales call, my parents invited me to go with them on a buying trip to New York. I was thrilled about this. Little did I realize that they had an ulterior motive. When we arrived in New York, we took a taxicab to the estate of a prominent diamond merchant. It was the largest house I had seen since arriving in America. The butler greeted us at the door and took us to a huge sitting room. In a few minutes the merchant, his wife, and an unusual looking girl who appeared to be in her twenties entered the room. Introductions were made and while my parents and the girl's parents interacted socially, the girl and I eyed each other in silence. After what seemed like an eternity, my parents and I left and checked into a hotel. My mother told me that they had made arrangements with the girl's parents for us to be married. I almost fainted! My father explained to me how wealthy this family was and her father had agreed that he would take me into his diamond business. I stood and exclaimed, "I have no intention of marrying that girl and there is no amount of money that would convince me otherwise." Mother said matter of factly, "Go ahead and marry her and in a few years after you get settled you can rent an apartment and get a mistress. That's the way that European men handle these matters. Think of your future, Peter." I was flabbergasted as I thought about Mother attempting to control the rest of my life through this "arrangement" that she and Father had made. I would not discuss the situation any further, which infuriated both of my parents. Again, I had refused to obey. They didn't say a word to me for a week or so. Finally, my father came to me and said that I was going to have to continue my career as a salesman with his company since I had refused what they viewed as "a golden opportunity."

The day before I was to leave on my first sales trip my

father gave me a lecture on discipline and hard work. He explained to me that the other salesmen worked on a four-teen percent commission; however, he decided that my commission would be twelve and a half percent. According to my father, this would give me incentive to be successful.

While out on the road, I made the usual mistakes of giv-ing too many discounts to crafty buyers, but I worked hard and soon became one of the most productive salesmen. I found that traveling on the road for sometimes two or three weeks at a time was hard, but at least it kept me away from my crappy home life. I covered over 60,000 miles a year and took very little time off.

Even though I was successful at my job, I was not happy. I hated living at home and my social life was almost non-existent. I had a few friends and dates from time to time, but no meaningful relationships.

One day, I received a chance telephone call from Meryl, a girl I had a crush on in high school. My very first date, the girl I dreamed of while in the service, was on the phone. She had just graduated from UCLA, where she majored in the-ater, and had come back to visit her family. We started dat-ing and before long, I fell in love. A few months later we got married in a small ceremony. Of course my parents disap-proved of my newfound happiness, but my faithful grand-mother welcomed my new wife into the family.

After my marriage, the job became harder and harder to tolerate; and after a grueling year on the road away from my wife most of the time, I asked my father if I could come off the road and work in the office. After all, he was always telling me the business would someday belong to me. He got angry and started to tell me about all the time he spent as a salesman. "If you don't want to be a salesman, I won't need you." We had a huge argument, both saying things we should not have said, and I ended up quitting. My father took my car away. His parting words were "Your Mother and I knew you would never amount to anything." I said to myself that I would prove them wrong.

* * *

Karla sat up. She saw the box lying on the floor. She reached over to pick it up and she saw that the word on the box had changed yet again. The word was Netsah. "Eternity, she whispered." She suddenly felt strong again and there was no pain. She stood up and looked through the window. She could not believe what she saw, for there before her was both Peter and Otto. They were side by side walking in unison. Their gaits were identical. But though they seemed so close there seemed to be a vast chasm between the mother and her son. She turned away and then she held the box up with both hands very close to her face. "Eternity! Eternity!" She knew the void between them was one of time and timelessness. She felt the presence of both her mother and her husband. Then they all turned and looked through the window together.

CHAPTER IX

*"The mystery of life is not a problem to be
solved, it is a reality to be lived."*
Van Der Leewarden

As soon as we arrived home, I checked with the hospital and everything was still as we had left it. Bonnie spent time with our grandchildren, and I spent the rest of the afternoon reading up my mail and periodically thinking about the events of the previous days. I now realized how hard it must have been for the doctor to make this kind of decision, not knowing whether she was killing someone by pulling the breathing tube. It was hard on everybody. The rest of Sunday was business as usual. On Monday morning I called the hospital and found out they had moved my mother out of intensive care and into a regular room. Her vital signs were still strong.

Bonnie and I took care of the things we needed to do and the remainder of Monday was a normal day. That evening I started feeling anxious, but I couldn't understand why. We had a quiet dinner and went to bed. At approximately 2:00AM, the phone rang. I caught it on the first ring because I had expected this call. The doctor was on the phone saying, "I'm sorry, Mr. Abeles, but your mother died in her sleep at 1:40AM Tuesday morning. Please let me know if I can do anything." He hung up and I stood there. She was gone. It didn't seem real. I went over to Bonnie and we simply held each other. Neither of us said a word. Finally, I spoke to say that I needed to make the arrangements. I slipped into automatic pilot. No time for emotion now; I must play the role of the good son. It was expected of me.

Bonnie reminded me that according to Jewish religion my mother had to be buried as soon as possible after death. I called the funeral home where they told me they could not pick her up from the hospital until they had a signed death certificate, and that they probably could not do this in time to have the funeral on Tuesday. They said we would probably have to schedule the funeral for Wednesday. I made all of the necessary phone calls finishing about 4:00AM There was no question in my mind that I would not be able to sleep anymore so I went down to my office and tried to do some work. Later in the morning, Bonnie and I got ready to return to New York. We both realized that we could not stay in my mother's apartment, so we stayed in the Hilton by the airport. It was a little inconvenient but at least there was a window at the hotel where I could stand and watch the cars go by. I saw a garbage truck weave its way in and out of the busy traffic below, and I was reminded of the strange but rewarding career path that I entered over forty years ago.

It was 1958, Heinz Robert had finished his post-doctoral work and had his first teaching position. He was an assistant professor at Ohio State University. Grandmother had gotten too old to live by herself. She was now at the Drexel Home for Aged Jews. I was unemployed, without a car, but determined to succeed.

As I perused the want ads, I realized that I needed to find a job where I would be furnished a car. There it was— "Wanted: Young man to handle collections. $60/week, plus car. Apply in person at Ace Scavenger Co." The next morning I was at their door before they opened. Dean Buntrock, their new general manager, interviewed me. I later learned that Dean had married one of the owner's daughters and had joined the family business. Dean capitalized on this break to become one of the most successful executives in the industry. He became the founder and first chief executive of Waste Management Inc.

Three days after my interview I was offered the collection job. I thought of this job as temporary and would continue to look for something better. In a few weeks it became apparent that this job offered a lot of opportunity. I put all my energy into being the first one at the office each day and the last to leave in the evening. I went to the office on Saturdays just to hang around and learn. After completing my regular work, I would pester everyone for assignments. My superiors soon noticed my ambition and hard work. I saw that the company had no salesmen. Either the drivers or the foreman would solicit new business. A suit and a tie were unheard of. After a few months, I asked Dean if I could go out and drum up new business. In a few days, I was given permission to start a sales program. We worked out a commission incentive and I loved it. I started to wear a suit and tie to work. Every chance I got I made sales calls. Construction was booming in Chicago. I started contacting builders and large commercial rental agencies. My sales program was succeeding, and soon I started getting substantial commission checks. My new career was on track.

One day Dean called me into his office. He told me that they had just bought a small, residential trash company and needed someone to manage it. Would I be interested? You bet! We agreed that I would manage this new company on weekends and receive an additional $50 per week. I was on cloud nine. What an opportunity!

By 1960, Meryl had found an interesting job with the Easter Seal Society and we were living in a nice apartment on the north side. The small suburban company I was managing had prospered and grown. The company had hired someone to take over my collection duties. This enabled me to spend all of my time managing the new company and working on the sales program. Everything was going well.

In February, my father started having serious health problems. He was too stubborn to admit that he was sorry I no longer worked for him. He often told Heinz Robert how proud he was of my accomplishments, but never told me.

It was a cold windy morning in March when I got the message on my two-way radio to call the office immediately. When I reached the office, they sadly informed me that my grandmother had died in her sleep that morning. I went to my parents' house, and my mother told me she was too upset over my father's health to handle the necessary arrangements. I would have to take care of everything. We called my brother and he said he would leave for Chicago as soon as he could. I was disturbed by my mother's attitude, but having no choice, I agreed to make the arrangements. I stopped by my wife's office on the way to the old age home. She was heartbroken and offered to go with me. I thanked her and told her I would need her support later. I would go alone. As I was driving to the home, I realized how much I loved my grandmother and how hard it would be to make her funeral arrangements. It came back to me. During all the years grandmother had been at the home, my parents never went to visit her. It was always my Grandmother who took public transportation to visit them. She would take a bus and the elevated train for a trip that lasted over an hour. It must have been so hard. I was glad that I had visited her weekly. When I arrived at the home, all of Grandmother's friends were waiting in the lobby to tell me how sorry they were and how much they would miss her. With a heavy heart, I cleaned out her room, made the funeral arrangements, and signed all of the required papers. Everyone wanted to know why I was there alone so I had to make some lame excuses.

The funeral was scheduled for the next morning. I went home where Meryl and I had a stiff drink, talked quietly, and waited for my brother to arrive. Heinz Robert and his wife came later that evening. I brought him up to date on the events of the day. He, too, was very upset that our Mother had not helped with the arrangements.

Meryl and I went to the funeral home early the next morning. I had to identify the body and take care of some last minute details. My mother, brother, and sister-in-law Barbara arrived shortly. Mother told me that my father was too ill to come and she was afraid it would be too much of a strain on him. There was a short service in the funeral home chapel before we left for the cemetery. As I listened to the rabbi at the grave side ceremony, I thought about my grandmother. I remembered her daily visits during my illness and how she used to make my favorite lunch. I recalled how she helped me with my homework all through high school and how she surprised us all a few years earlier when she announced, "Today I became a citizen." She was eighty years old at the time. I was extremely sad and tried hard to keep my composure. After the funeral, Meryl and I spent the rest of the day with my brother and his wife. I did not want to see my parents. I was deeply hurt and disappointed with the way they handled the death of Grandmother.

The next few weeks were very difficult. I was terribly depressed. I continued to do my job, but the fire was gone. Meryl noticed how sad and despondent I was, so one night after dinner, we had a long talk. She told me that she was not happy either. She missed Los Angeles and show business. She reminded me that I had promised to go to L.A. with her if she became homesick. She also felt a change of scenery would be good for my depression. Our discussion made a lot of sense to me. I was disenchanted with my parents and my brother was living in Ohio. I resigned my position with Ace Scavenger and we left for the West Coast.

I chuckled, a young couple living the glamorous life in Southern California seemed like such a ridiculously positive thought at this juncture of my life.

Why did I seem to be so devoid of negative emotion? I was going to place my mother in the ground and she would no longer be an active participant in my story. Yet, I wasn't all that sad. I wanted to cry but I could not. Suddenly, it occurred to me that with my father and grandmother gone as well, I was virtually the last remnant of that Austrian dynasty. Heinz Robert was ill and I had no one to connect me with that boy in the window but myself. I was suddenly cold and I climbed into bed and felt the warmth of Bonnie beside me. I slept, but not without nightmares from those ghosts of my past.

I entered a world of men in black uniforms shouting orders and of beautiful Austrian women with cold dark stares demanding gentlemanly behavior. I screamed, but everyone laughed. Just when I felt that I could not take any more pain or ridicule, my grandmother appeared and held me close to her and ever so gently shooed them all away. They all left immediately and there was peace. I said proudly that I loved her, she smiled and I fell asleep in her arms. I felt so warm. The alarm clock on the nightstand beeped relentlessly and I awoke slowly from the night's restless slumber. I began a brand new day not understanding that beginnings are merely a place to start.

* * *

Karla turned first to look at her husband and then to look at her mother. They were both smiling. Then she spoke to Peter. "Eternity is real, Peter. We really do have forever. You must always believe that, my son." Then a tear rolled down her cheek.

The Abeles Apartment Building
(the entire floor)

Father's Automobile

Heinz Robert, Peter Otto, and Mother

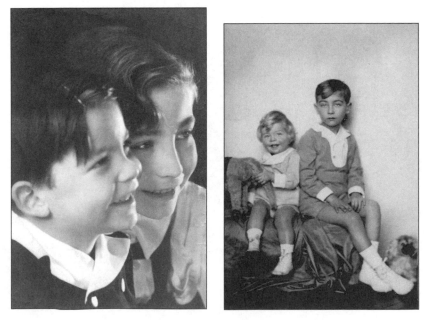

The Abeles Brothers

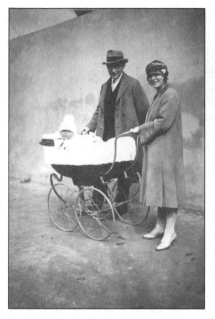

Father and Mother with
baby Otto

Parents on Honeymoon
Monte Carlo 1920s

Grandmother

Grandfather

Vacationing at Summer Home
Baden by Vien
1935-1936

SS *Rotterdam*

This was my Mother's travel pass for the train ride when she left Austria

Karla Abeles, age 27

Chicago school picture

The Abeles family at dinner 1945

Heinz Robert
training for
counterintelligence

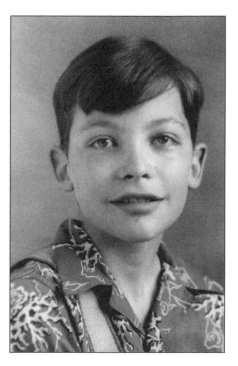

Peter Otto as a Patrol boy

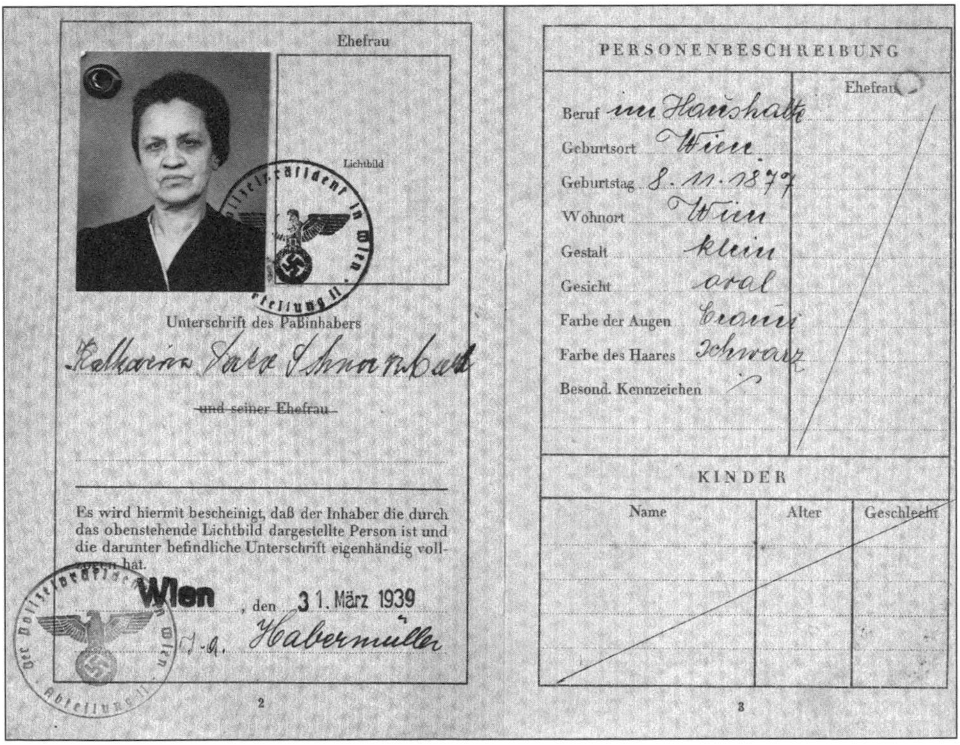

Ehefrau

Lichtbild

Polizeipräsident in Wien Abteilung II

Unterschrift des Paßinhabers

Katharina Sara Schnabel

~~und seiner Ehefrau~~

Es wird hiermit bescheinigt, daß der Inhaber die durch das obenstehende Lichtbild dargestellte Person ist und die darunter befindliche Unterschrift eigenhändig vollzogen hat.

Wien, den 31. März 1939

I.A. Habermüller

2

PERSONENBESCHREIBUNG

		Ehefrau
Beruf	im Haushalt	
Geburtsort	Wien	
Geburtstag	8.11.1877	
Wohnort	Wien	
Gestalt	klein	
Gesicht	oval	
Farbe der Augen	braun	
Farbe des Haares	schwarz	
Besond. Kennzeichen	—	

KINDER

Name	Alter	Geschlecht

3

This was my grandmother's travel pass when she left Austria

UNITED STATES
HEADQUARTERS BERLIN DISTRICT
Berlin, Germany

Office of the A. C. of S., G-2

APO 755, US Army

25 March 1946

COMMENDATION

T/5 ABELES, Robert, BDID, is commended for his excellent work in connection with the apprehension of Mildred GILLARS, a U.S. citizen, better known as "AXIS SALLY" who was broadcasting for the Germans during the war.

Based on a well designed plan of his own, T/5 ABELES, with cleverness and endurance, learned subject's whereabouts, and by closely following up all available clues, finally succeeded in tracking subject down, to apprehend her, and to turn her over to representatives of the Department of Justice.

T/5 ABELES worked untiringly and displayed great skill in carrying out his highly important mission.

C. A. BUECHNER
Lt. Col., GSC
A.C. of S., G-2

Otto in the Air Force with his buddies

No. 78-640

In the
Supreme Court of the United States

OCTOBER TERM, 1978

UNITED STATES OF AMERICA EX REL. PETER O. ABELES,

Petitioner,

vs.

RICHARD J. ELROD, SHERIFF OF
COOK COUNTY, ILLINOIS,

Respondent.

PETITIONER'S REPLY BRIEF IN SUPPORT OF
CERTIORARI PETITION

JEROLD S. SOLOVY
ROBERT L. GRAHAM
TERRY ROSE SAUNDERS
One IBM Plaza
Chicago, Illinois 60611
(312) 222-9350
Attorneys for Petitioner

Of Counsel:
JENNER & BLOCK

UNITED STATES LAW PRINTING CO., CHICAGO, ILLINOIS 60618 (312) 525-6581

THE WELCH FOUNDATION 1995 AWARD BANQUET

HONORING

DR. ROBERT H. ABELES

AND

DR. JEREMY R. KNOWLES

The co-recipients of the 1995 Robert A. Welch Award in Chemistry are leaders in the field of enzyme chemistry. Both have added greatly to our understanding of how enzymes function in helping carry out the multitude of chemical reactions in a living system. The two scientists' basic research also has helped lay a foundation for the enormous potential enzymes hold in the treatment of disease.

Bonnie, Otto and Heinz Robert
in Naples, Florida

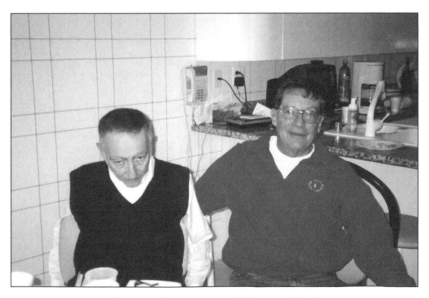

Heinz Robert and Otto, 1998

My Family

Chapter X

"Not I - Not anyone else, can travel that
road for you.
You must travel it for yourself"
Walt Whitman

I walked to the window of my hotel. I loved looking out windows. I had been doing it all my life. It was a warm sunny day in late May. Long Island was pretty this time of year. This was an important day for me. Today I would bury my mother.

My name is Peter Otto Abeles, and at sixty eight years of age, I have concluded that every event of my life holds the key to the treasure box of understanding how God works, where do people, friends and foes, fit in, and why my self-worth must never be defined by circumstances or material possessions. The boy in my mind and the man in my mirror are one and the same, unified in this earthly adventure; unwilling to forget, eager to forgive, and ready to love whatever appears through the window of life, or so I thought.

* * *

"I have the treasure box, Peter," Karla screamed. She held it up to the window and as she raised it she noticed that the word "Kabbalah" had reappeared on the top of the box. It didn't look like gold script anymore. It looked as if it were written in fire.

"We are receiving a great treasure, you and I, Peter, together."

"Are you enjoying the gift, Karla?" Ezekiel asked as she lowered the box and turned around.

"Oh, yes, I am. It's priceless, Ezekiel."

"Would you like to take a walk with me now, Karla?"

"No, Ezekiel, I think I shall stay here by the window."

"Very well, Karla. I will see you soon."

"Goodbye," she said as she spun around to see swirling flakes of powdery snow dancing around the outside of her window pane.

CHAPTER XI

*"In the beginner's mind there are many possi-
bilities, but in the expert's there are few."*
Shunryu Suzuki

The city of Vienna was covered with a dusting of early winter snow. "If she asks me to kill myself again," I mused, "I will run away to the place I've read about where dreams come true." The name resonated in my head, "Hollywood." I knew nothing about it, only that it was about make-believe, a place where there was always a happy ending. For me, the gray tones of the city below were invisible. The window no longer represented a clear glass portal between inside and outside, but a bridge between ugliness and beauty, between reality and dreams. I cried like always and placed my hands upon the pane, this time pushing until the glass broke from the pressure. The shards of glass seemed to scream as they flew seemingly in slow motion to the street below. I looked at my bleeding hands and watched my blood drop to the street below. Surprisingly, my crying stopped and the corners of my lips slowly turned upward. My grandmother gasped to see the smiling, bloody figure of young Otto with eyes closed, seemingly frozen in time and space.

My eyes opened and I blinked repeatedly until I convinced myself that I was safe from the clutches of the worst nightmare since my mother's funeral. Two weeks had past since that life-changing event. "I'm just getting comfortable with this forgiveness thing. Now what?" I must have spoken the words aloud because I felt Bonnie stir. I held my left index finger to my own lips and whispered "shhh." She settled down and the familiar sleep sound of her breathing convinced me that my conversation with myself would remain private. Just to be sure, I tiptoed out of the bedroom, grabbing my bathrobe that was lying on the foot of the bed. I made a pot of decaf-feinated coffee and sat at the kitchen table. I looked at the clock…4:00A.M. The word, "Hollywood," kept echoing through my mind. Two cups of coffee later the assault inside my head had not stopped.

"Mother, help me. Help me like you did before!" My hands were shaking, fearful that I would hear the voice again, yet desiring it above all else. *"Otto, we aren't finished. I must help you. You do trust me, don't you?"*

"I have forgiven you, don't you remember?" I asked.

"Yes, but that was not my question. Do you trust me?" she asked.

I suddenly rose from my chair and walked to the kitchen window without answering.

"You tried running once, didn't you, Otto? Did it work then? Think about it."

I started to answer, but didn't. I knew there was no one there to hear me.

I remembered another time when a young man learned his first adult lesson in Hollywood. My first wife Meryl and I drove across the United States in three days. The trip to the West Coast was filled with talk of beginning a new life together. She was a petite redhead with beautiful green eyes and a captivating smile. She was a look-alike for Shirley McClaine. Her bubbly personality and great sense of humor made the long hours of driving pass by quickly. As we put distance between Chicago and us, I started to feel free and soon realized it was mostly because I was away from the influence of my parents, or so I thought.

It was just another sunny day in Southern California when we arrived in Hollywood. We checked into a motel on Sunset Boulevard with a pink exterior and the mandatory palm trees out front. I opened the door to room 128 and dropped the bags to the floor. I had never been in a room so full of light. As we made love, I felt as though I was finally calling the shots. After changing into a pair of Bermuda shorts and my recently acquired aloha shirt, we began to explore a new magical kingdom where ordinary people became stars. It was like being on a movie set where everything was make-believe. Meryl was in her element. After staying in the motel for a few days, we located a one-bedroom pool apartment near the corner of Hollywood Boulevard and Vine Street. What a great location it was! Since we were both exhausted from all the sightseeing and had not had a "real" honeymoon, we decided to take a few days off and relax Hollywood-style. We sat by the pool during the day acquiring tans while sightseeing and dancing all night. I sensed that Meryl would never leave California again. I was going to try to make L.A. my new home as well. Then reality came into the picture.

Meryl became restless before I did and she started looking at the want ads in the local paper. She was determined to be involved with the film industry and had decided she would like to go into casting for a career. She arranged several job interviews; and for the first time in my life, I was willing to sit around and do nothing. Meryl encouraged me to take my time and decide what I really wanted to do. After a few interviews, she landed a job as an assistant casting director at 20th Century Fox Studio. I had never seen her happier. It was bittersweet because I knew I would have to share her with the studio.

My desire for gainful employment soon returned and I took a series of jobs ranging from selling photo-copy machines to selling advertising, though none of these jobs lasted very long, especially the position as a copy machine salesman. I managed to spill photocopy solution on an attorney's white rug during my very first sales call. None of my explanations seemed to appease my boss and I quickly found myself looking for another job. Needless to say, these unglamorous positions didn't build up my male ego. My previous experience with Ace Scavenger in Chicago helped me land a job with a garbage company called Fleet Disposal. I hated to say it, but it was great to be back in the garbage business again. It was as if I was saying to my parents, "I won't take the easy or predictable road to success. No, not me! I'll select a business where people's trash, their disposable items, their worthless unwanted things can be transformed into something of value for an enterprising lad. I'll find a safe and comfortable home where no one else wants to be."

We moved into a large two-bedroom apartment located in West L.A. near the university. Meryl was successful in her new job and was ardently striving to work her way to the top. She beamed with enthusiasm. Since I had few friends in California, our social life revolved around show business personalities. At first, it was exciting meeting and socializing with such celebrities as Carol Burnett, Charles Laughton, and Peter Falk, who were genuinely interesting people. However, I soon realized just how superficial and self-centered most of our new friends and acquaintances really were. Actually, my new acquaintances weren't nearly as shallow or phony as I was. I loved Meryl immensely but there was no way I could be the husband she wanted me to be, here in California. This was her kingdom, not mine. I remember one Christmas eve when Meryl asked me to rent a U-Haul trailer and attach it to our car for delivering and receiving gifts for her and her Hollywood friends. I had resorted to playing Santa Claus. Thank goodness she didn't ask me to put on a red suit and white beard. My fantasy world turned out to be another disappointment. I was beginning to resent my own wife and my inability to be in control of the finances and our social calendar. How could I ever prove to my mother and father how great I was…here? I was pretending that miles could separate me from my dragons. That was impossible. Incrementally, the passion of two young lovers on a common journey gave way to disgusted strangers clumsily avoiding any intimate contact. The marriage ended physically first then died a slow emotional death within two years after we arrived in California. I was suffering from depression. I didn't want to get up in the mornings. I envied Meryl's enthusiasm and detested my lack of it. This simply couldn't go on. So one morning, Meryl blew me a last kiss as she left for work, and I just stood there feeling as lonely and awkward as the day we left Grandmother at the railway station in Vienna.

I stood at our apartment window and looked down at the pool that afternoon remembering earlier joyous times of delicious cocktails, warm sun, and talk of sharing the rest of our lives in this paradise together. Now I felt empty, but relieved and I knew Meryl was feeling relief too. I hadn't been a good husband. It was time for me to go. The same feeling of having to start over again crept into my mind as I remembered when I left Vienna. I began to cry and I wondered if my life would be a series of empty good-byes and unrealized dreams. I remember thinking while packing my suitcases that since there was no animosity on either side the divorce would be fast and uncomplicated. "Run, Otto, Run!" A voice inside my mixed-up head screamed. Then I remembered the lesson that my father had taught me. Work hard, don't get emotionally attached, and make money. Make lots of money. Buy yourself a little happiness along the way.

The next thing I remember was sitting behind the wheel of my 1957 Eldorado Baritz convertible heading East toward Chicago.

"That was a hell of a car," I whispered to myself. Then I stood at "attention," a throwback to my Air Force days and said matter of factly, "Okay, Mother. Those were some bitter-sweet memories and I'm honest enough to say I don't know if I trust you or my own feelings enough to go to all the other scary places in my past, but I'll try. Okay? So the little boy in the man's body ran away to California to play husband in Lala land and he couldn't make the grade. But I cut my losses early and came back. I learned my lesson, didn't I?" The silence was deafening.

* * *

Karla was silent. She watched Peter through the window but she didn't say a word. She didn't know what to say. She looked down at the box and there was no word at all on top.

"Madam, your car is ready."

Karla stood and turned toward the voice. She knew she recognized it.

"Madam, your car is ready."

"Adolph, is that you?" asked Karla.

"Yes, of course, I thought you would like to take your usual drive," replied Adolph. "That sounds fantastic, Adolph, let's do it. He had shined the black car and Karla suddenly realized she had on her favorite dress, the black one with gold buttons and trim. On her finger was the ring that Ernst had given her the day he asked her to be his wife. Adolph opened the door to the car and Karla got in the back. Lying on the seat next to her was a bouquet of her favorite flowers. And there was the black box as well. On the top of the box was a very short word, "Hod," which she knew meant splendor. As Adolph drove her through the streets of her familiar Vienna, she did indeed relive the splendor.

CHAPTER XII

"Thoughts are things"
Napoleon Hill

"Adolph, when will I drive this car?" I asked pointedly as my driver brought me home from school. Adolph's lean face turned sideways so I could see his craggy features from the back seat. A cigarette dangled from his thin lips. "The moment you are man enough to press the accelerator, Otto." Adolph laughed and turned to face the afternoon traffic and gave me the best ride of my life...

...until twenty five years later when I hit the Illinois state line doing 130 m.p.h., top back on the Eldorado, with Sinatra crooning on the radio. I had purchased my big white Cadillac from the manager of the Hollywood Roosevelt Hotel. Unfortunately, I blew the transmission as I passed the city limit sign heading into Chicago in the spring of 1962. From a pay phone, while waiting for a tow truck, I contacted my old employer, Dean Buntrock, and asked about the possibility of returning to my previous position. I crossed my fingers while I awaited his response. He politely told me he would find a place for me in his organization. I concealed my excitement as I arranged a meeting time. Even though I had not spoken to my parents for two years, I called to let them know I had returned to Chicago to resume my career. They sounded truly glad to hear from me and interested to know what had been going on in my life. They asked me to move in with them, thank goodness! I was amazed and somewhat baffled, as they had never expressed that much concern before. I tried to get into a detailed discussion with my father about his health and the family business, but it was clear that he didn't want to discuss either subject. It seemed as though every time I tried

101

to get into a serious conversation with him he would rebuff me. I recalled that years ago when I first started working for him we would go out onto the balcony, light up cigarettes, and talk shop. That was about as close to a loving relationship as I could ever expect with him. I came to the startling realization that I really did not know this man—my own Father. "All he does, Ernst, is stare out that window. It's not healthy. You've got to put a stop to it. I can't endure his aloofness." Mother spoke loudly so I would hear her complaint. "I shall speak to the boy," my Father declared, then he walked to the window where I sat. He spoke sternly, "Otto, you are upsetting your mother. Don't you realize what she is going through? The men in this family must assume their responsibilities. That includes Heinz Robert and yourself." He grabbed my shoulders and squeezed firmly, "Do you understand?" I nodded but my gut tightened and the voices in my head refrained, "No, I do not understand!"

I telephoned my brother to let him know I was back home and found out he had left Ohio State for a better position at Michigan State. A full professorship was just around the corner. As always, speaking with him was an encouragement and he wished me the best of luck. "Nothing will stop us as long as we stick together, Otto." I thought I heard him say, but the receiver was already on the cradle.

My father was a large, strong, robust man but I realized after seeing him that his health was deteriorating. He was gaunt and his shoulders were slumped. Not since the day his business was taken had he looked like this. When he left the room Mother told me that he had a slow spreading cancer. He would not admit it, but his friends had told Mother it was becoming much more difficult for him to manage his business. He finally confided in me after much prodding that he was thinking about selling the business and moving to New York to be close to his brother Felix. My mother was her old self, egotistical and suspicious of both my father and me, not supportive of us having one-on-one conversations. Even the relationship I had with my father was shaped by my mother's manipulative personality. Whether it was jealousy or bitterness, there was not going to be enough room in their household for the three of us for very long.

I spent as little time at home as possible and more time enjoying the city that I loved. It was great to be back in Chicago. I had forgotten how exciting it was with its colorful Mayor Daley making headlines every day. While reading The Chicago Tribune one day, a story appeared that he had gotten upset at an alderman who was speaking in opposition to one of Daley's programs at a recent city council meeting. Since Daley had the mechanical capability to turn off any microphone in the council chamber at his discretion, he abruptly silenced the offending member's microphone and continued with the meeting. I loved local politics. I had fun calling my old friends and former business associates to let them know I was back in town and dying to catch up with what was happening in their lives. Every Old Style Beer tasted great and the red hots were as wonderful as I remembered. However, as I would look out the window of my parents' apartment late at night after they were asleep, I realized that time was widening the gap between my parents and myself. I could not find solace in their arms and I no longer had a wife. The only thing that kept me going emotionally was the memory of my dear, sweet grandmother. I missed her terribly. Throughout my entire life, I had relied on her loving kindness even when she was in the old age home. The weekly visits I made to her as a young man provided me with the strength to carry on.

I kept my appointment with Dean Buntrock and the minute I walked into the Ace Scavenger office I felt at home, and everyone was glad to see me again. During my meeting with Dean that lasted the rest of the day, I learned that there had been a lot of growth in this vibrant company. They had made several acquisitions, including a major industrial hauling company in Milwaukee, Wisconsin. Much had changed since I left Chicago. There had been tremendous improvements in technology and operating equipment.

Then a new door opened for me. Dean told me that he would like to start a new company to be called City Disposal Company in Wisconsin. As the baby boomers began to acquire wealth and housing, the amount of trash they produced grew exponentially. This new company that Dean told me about was to specialize in municipal contract hauling, focusing on servicing individual homes and small businesses. I was to live in Milwaukee and get the new company off the ground. There would be a transitional time for me. At first, I would spend two days in Chicago working on sales and the other five days in Wisconsin. The plan was that I would rent and work out of an apartment in Milwaukee. As soon as the company got some business, we would open a real office and I would be in charge. I would always be grateful to Dean for providing me with this opportunity in my professional life. The greater thanks, however, would be for the faith he placed in me, something I had never received from my family. I now knew that I was special, that I had a talent, and I was going to prove to the world that I would be successful. We shook hands to consummate the deal, and I could hardly wait to get going. Being a self-starter, I dove in with both feet. I stayed in Chicago long enough to set up a viable sales program then hopped in my car, drove to Milwaukee, rented an austere apartment, and started calling on municipalities.

This new beginning was like the fresh start I received as a boy many years before when I returned to class after my life-threatening illness and wondered if anyone would remember me. As I entered the classroom, the entire class left their seats and ran to me. My teacher shook my small hands and said enthusiastically, "It's so good to have you back." I beamed and then proceeded to thank each of my classmates but thought to myself, "It's so good to be here." My mother inquired that evening about my day at school and I simply said, "It was fine!"

* * *

Karla stepped out of the car and told Adolph she would call him when she needed him again. The car sped away and slowly disappeared. She walked silently over to the window and spoke to Peter in a very cheerful voice. "Ahh, yes, Peter, we both had splendid days from time to time, didn't we? Life offers those beautiful beginnings and opportunities so that we can find out what we are truly capable of. A mother's greatest joy is watching the lives of her children unfold."

CHAPTER XIII

*"All the world loves a winner, and
has no time for a loser."*
Knute Rockne

There were so many opportunities for me that it made my new job exciting. It wasn't long before I was working twelve hours a day, seven days a week. I was driven to make this company the best in the United States. In Chicago, I called on all my old contacts, especially the commercial real estate companies. I felt most at home when I was in front of a customer, past or prospective.

One of my best contacts was a young vice president at a company called Arthur Rubeloff and Company. He was an enthusiastic man named Don LeBold. His company managed an enormous portfolio of new properties in the city. He and I became fast friends and started seeing each other at social events as well as professionally. One night he introduced me to a young lady named Sandra J. Allweiss. It was love at first sight for the second time. She was smart and had a fantastic outgoing personality. Talking with her was wonderful. For the first time in many months, my attention was turned to something other than business. I had buried myself in my career and I suddenly realized that I was lonely for an emotional and physical relationship. I asked Sandra for a date and to my surprise, she accepted. The next few weeks we saw each other a lot, and I realized that I was ready to try marriage again. I had visions of a little house with a green lawn and an Irish setter standing by the front door in anticipation of my arrival for supper. All it took was money, I supposed.

Years earlier, I remember walking into my room after seeing the German soldiers marching down the street in front of our apartment. I had my own toy soldiers strategically placed in neat little rows on a table in the corner. I liked order and discipline. My room was tidy, as usual, and I talked to my tin minions, "You are good little soldiers. If you obey me, I will take very good care of you." I surveyed my kingdom and saluted my troops not realizing at the time that my strategies would be used when I grew up.

My hard work paid off and as the year progressed, my sales efforts in Chicago were fruitful. Wisconsin produced a lot of prospects but sales were a little sluggish. I guess it was because I was not a local guy. I wasn't discouraged, though, and just kept plugging away. The old Abeles tenacity was coming in handy. If there was anything my life had taught me it was to never give up and I was not ever going to return to my parents' house as a failure.

I recalled that fateful day in Vienna of my school's geography bee. I faced my opponent, Karl, in the contest. He had correctly identified Copenhagen as the capital of Denmark. This put me in second place. I accepted my second place ribbon with honor and shook hands vigorously with Karl, congratulating my tall blond opponent. I couldn't wait to tell my parents. Their response that afternoon was not what I expected. Mother spoke up, while Father quietly nodded, "Otto, maybe next time I'll be able to tell my friends about your first place ribbon. Keeping working hard, son." "Yes, Mother," I replied politely feeling as if a dagger was piercing my heart.

One day while driving through one of Milwaukee's industrial neighborhoods looking for business, I saw a dump truck carrying industrial trash. It was departing from one of the large gates at American Motors, a huge automotive assembly plant. I could hardly believe that with all of the new technology that was available, they were still using dump trucks to remove their waste. I called them to discuss their trash removal program. As a shark smells blood, I could smell opportunity here. I was looking for the right account to introduce the newest piece of equipment available. The "stationary compactor" was brand new back then. This was an untried machine, capable of producing a four-to-one compaction ratio. This was unheard of at that time. I was so pumped up that I was able to get the purchasing people at American Motors to be as excited about this product as I was and they agreed to a trial installation. The manufacturer, Anchor Pack, agreed to give us a machine for ninety days free of charge. It was a real coup. The first day of the trial, I stayed at the plant for twenty-four hours. I just wanted to make sure everything went perfectly. At the end of the ninety-day period, I landed a three-year contract. I was ecstatic and went out and bought myself a bottle of champagne, as this was the largest account I had ever gotten. When Dean Buntrock handed me a $5,000.00 bonus, I nearly went through the roof. My confidence was soaring and I called on more accounts than ever before.

As the year 1962 drew to a close, I gave up my work in Chicago, and started working full-time in Wisconsin. I got myself a fantastic office with a big window so I could look out and survey my kingdom, one of trash; but my kingdom nonetheless. Then the municipal sector of my business began to pay off. I was very close to getting my first municipal contract with a small city near Madison. Soon my dream of managing my own disposal company, the City Disposal Company, would be a reality.

The year 1963 started out with a bang. We signed our first municipal contract in the city of Stoughton, Wisconsin. Life became hectic for me. Trucks were ordered, a land fill had to be prepared, and employees hired. As far as I was concerned, the more work the better. I stood by my window often in the late evening and looked out at the lights. I thought to myself, whether it's Vienna, Chicago, or Milwaukee, standing by the window was my source of energy. I guess you could say it's the way I recharge my batteries.

* * *

Karla raised her hand to the glass and touched it, wishing she could stroke Peter's hair. She suddenly felt someone place hands on her head and gently pat it. "Who is it?" she asked as she turned.

"Karla, it is me, Franz." He had been a playmate and she hadn't seen him since they were fifteen-years-old. His family had moved away to Berlin and Karla had never really forgotten him. He was a very athletic boy with broad shoulders, a big smile, and close-cropped light blond hair. He had told Karla many times that he was going to marry her and she believed that. Then he moved away and she thought about him from time to time until she met Ernst and began her new life. After that, thoughts of Franz slowly melted away until the Anschluss. After the Anschluss she began to have dreams of Franz far away in the heart of Germany, crying out for her to help him. There was not a single thing she could do. "I am so sorry, Franz," for she knew his fate. She began to sob. He touched her cheek with his hands.

"Now, now, there was nothing you could do. Don't worry, I'm very happy here," and he stepped back and stood tall. He always had such impeccable manners and he always spoke so beautifully. The cut of his clothes always flattered his stately appearance even as a boy of fifteen. Then Franz was gone. She turned to the window and she could see a wedding and there was Peter in his black tuxedo standing next to Ernst, father and son. "Yes, Ernst, you gave me a beautiful son and I am so grateful."

CHAPTER XIV

*"It's been a hard day's night, and I've been
working like a dog."*

The Beatles

Sandra and I decided to get married on April 25, 1963. We toasted to eternal love. I thought to myself that for me, eternity was somewhat fluid. While I was drinking champagne, my mother was up to her old tricks again. She pulled Sandra to the side and gave her what she considered to be sage advice. "Sandra," Mother said, "if my son doesn't do what you want him to do, just don't let him sleep with you, and in a few days he will begin to see things your way. Trust me, I know men." After Sandra told me about this conversation, I wondered how often this technique was used on my father. I vowed I would never be manipulated in this manner. After the honeymoon, there were not enough hours in the day it seemed, but somehow everything was accomplished. My personal life appeared to be in order and my professional life was booming. Life was good for me and I was extremely happy in those days.

In 1964, Heinz Robert became a full professor at Brandeis University. Then the two most wonderful events of my life occurred. On May 29, 1964, Bryan Scott Abeles, my son, was born and on September 30, 1965, Michelle Catherine Abeles was born. Like all new fathers do, I made a commitment that I would provide them with the best life possible, and I continued to work day into night. For the next three years, my career advanced steadily. City Disposal grew rapidly as I signed up many more municipalities and new industrial accounts. We moved from Milwaukee to Kenosha because I had gotten another American Motors plant. As our business grew, there were many problems with personnel, equipment, and landfills, but it was fun solving them. During these busy times, I saw very little of my parents. One night as I sat and sipped a cup of coffee and looked out my living room window, I thought about my father. His health was getting worse, and he had finally decided to sell his business. My brother and I tried to help him financially from time to time since his failing health had affected his income. We felt that it was our duty as sons, ingrained in us from the time when we had the paper route back in Chicago.

I became stressed when I couldn't accomplish both the work I needed to perform in the office and make the outside sales calls to acquire new business and service my existing accounts. The telephone company helped solve my problem by introducing a new device called a mobile phone. They were not very sophisticated in the early days, consisting of an ugly black box with a rotary dial that was attached to the floor between the driver and passenger seat. It was a good thing that cars were made larger in those days to accommodate this monstrosity. The only way I could make or receive a call was through the mobile operator. After having the phone for only a few days, I took Bryan to nursery school one morning. As I pulled out of the parking lot, I received a call. It was one of my suppliers who was having a delivery problem that would affect one of my biggest customers. In the middle of a heated discussion, I didn't notice that the traffic light had turned from green to red and proceeded through the intersection where I immediately collided with an approaching car. No one was seriously injured, but my car was totaled, except for the telephone, which was still working. In the middle of smoke and crushed metal I could hear my supplier screaming. I learned a valuable lesson about talking on a phone while driving which has stayed with me until this day.

By the end of that year, things were under control in Kenosha and we moved to Madison. My parents had made their decision to move to New York. By now, the operation in

Wisconsin was a full-time job. City Disposal was becoming a well-known entity throughout the state. In 1970, a full-page article appeared in the Madison State Journal, a prominent newspaper. The entire story was about City Disposal and me, Pete Abeles. I had carved out a niche in this business, and I exuded confidence.

In June 1970, Ace Scavenger and a group of affiliated companies went public and became Waste Management. I remember trying to get friends and relatives to buy stock in this new corporation. They all said, "Who would want to own stock in a garbage company?" The stock went from 5.25 to 80.0 in a very short period of time. This company made many men wealthy. For the next two years, I continued to run City Disposal's Wisconsin operations. Waste Management bought a large competitor, Eckles Sanitation. While I was excited about the buy-out, this really increased my responsibilities. Further, from time to time, Dean Buntrock would ask me to take on special assignments in various parts of the country. Needless to say, I had a very full plate. The assignment I enjoyed the most was when I got to go to Florida to work with Wayne Huizinga. He was such a dynamic person and, like me, enjoyed working seven days a week. I could feel how ambitious he was and could sense that he was going to be successful in all of his endeavors. Little did I know that he would later own Blockbuster Video, the Miami Dolphins, the Florida Marlins, a hockey team in Florida, Auto Nation, and Republic Services. Boy, did I call that one correctly! I secretly wished I could live in Florida and work for him exclusively.

At the same time, Heinz Robert was making a name for himself. He was appointed chairman of the graduate department of biochemistry at Brandeis. Meanwhile, Waste Management had decided to get into the waste paper recycling business, and my life was changed forever. They were negotiating to buy the waste paper division of the Lissner Corporation, commonly called Paper Recovery. Both the Lissner Corporation and the new Paper Recovery division were located on historic Goose Island. The island is located between the two branches of the Chicago River near the infamous, often dangerous, public-housing project known as Cabrini Green. This was a Chicago industrial area where the elevated trains ran overhead and railroad tracks criss-crossed with empty freight cars everywhere in a continu-ously changing neighborhood. This subsidiary was run by one of the Lissner brothers, Meyer Lissner. Since no one at Waste Management had any experience in the recycling industry, they hired a consultant by the name of Ed Law, a bright young engineer with a business background. At the time this was all happening, I had no idea how much impact Meyer Lissner and Ed Law would have on the rest of my life. When the final negotiations were completed, it was decided that I should move back to the Chicago area, which didn't disappoint me at all. I still considered Chicago my home. I was to learn the recycling business and eventually become president of the new division. I liked the sound of that, "President." It sounded powerful and important. My father and mother would be proud of me; at least I imagined they would be. I put our Madison home up for sale, turned City Disposal over to an assistant, and found a house in the northern suburb of Chicago, Northbrook. After settling in, I flew to Minneapolis, Minnesota, to meet my new boss, Ed Law. While on the plane I remember looking out the window and reflecting on my life. My parents had moved to New York and had rented the apartment I would later grow to hate. My father had managed to find a job as an accountant and my brother was at the peak of his career. Everything was perfect, except my marriage was falling apart. I sus-pected that my wife had developed a serious drinking prob-lem. I felt helpless in identifying the root causes for whatev-er troubled Sandra. She couldn't tell me, or more likely, I couldn't listen. I did not like hearing bad news at home. It just was not acceptable. I compensated by completely turn-ing away from her. Unfortunately, our innocent children suf-fered inadvertently from our inability to cope with the complex issues of our relationship. My troubled past was filled with incidents where turning away from problems was the only course of action that I could conceive.

Professionally, I could sense a new and exciting phase that my life was about to begin. It seemed contradictory that I would be rising while someone else was falling into loneliness and despair. I suppose that as I looked out my windows. I chose to imagine that it wasn't happening, that my "wonderland" wasn't really falling apart.

As I got off the plane in Minneapolis, I had no trouble spotting Ed Law in the waiting area. I had been given a detailed description of him. He was a dashing figure dressed like a college professor and he had the credentials to go with the looks. He had an engineering degree from the University of Michigan and a masters degree from the Wharton School of Business. As we got into his car, he took out a huge cigar and offered me one. This was a good omen. One of the greatest pleasures I have had in life is smoking cigars. Ed and I liked each other immediately, and in a short while it seemed we had known each other all our lives. I was glad to have a new friend, and came to consider Ed to be more like a brother. I didn't get to see Heinz Robert very often. Ed and I spent the next two days discussing how we would manage the new company that was about to be acquired. When I got home the transaction was completed and Waste Management owned a paper recycling company. I was officially in the paper recycling business.

I set up shop at the Lissner Corporation office and started to learn this brand new business. We decided that in order for it to grow properly and to prosper, a new plant was needed. This industry was much more exciting than the trash business. We were able to make money and recycle, which was becoming a popular trend in this country. The plant itself was a small portion of the business. The brokerage, or the buying and selling of wastepaper, was the crux of the operation. It was so exciting to be sitting in the office buying tons and tons of waste paper and selling and shipping it to a third party. I loved it. Meyer Lissner was a master and he loved teaching the tricks of the trade to a young protégé like myself. He had become a surrogate father to me. In a short period of time I had acquired both a surrogate brother and a father. These people actually respected and valued my opinions. I was at an all-time high. The Lissner Corporation was a huge company but the atmosphere in that office was very pleasant, almost intimate in nature. There were phones everywhere, even in the bathrooms. Nobody went out to lunch because they had a complete kitchen staffed with a full-time cook and a person who served us. There were wonderful four-course lunches everyday, and if the Lissner brothers decided to work late, which happened frequently, dinner was also served. It was like one big happy family. I certainly wasn't accustomed to that, and soon I was on the phone, wheeling and dealing and making lots of money for this new company. By the time our new plant was finished, Meyer Lissner was letting me do almost all of the trading. He would analyze each transaction after I hung up the phone. It was a great way to learn. I confided to Meyer that I was frustrated and wished that I could own my own business. I had come to the conclusion that it was hard to accumulate any wealth while working for someone else. He cautioned me to just be patient and he always said, "Kid, your time will come. Just wait and grab it when it happens." One of the most important things Meyer did was to introduce Ed Law and me to the Golden Ox Restaurant. This was a fantastic place to eat and socialize. The Golden Ox was located a few blocks from our office and both of us fell in love with this place the minute we entered the front door. It was very old fashioned with a huge oak bar; wooden tables with checkered tablecloths; and plump, friendly waitresses dressed in authentic German costumes. The menu had all of my favorite German dishes, including delicious veal dishes and goulash made from prime beef chunks mixed with cubed potatoes in thick brown gravy. Not since my boyhood when Grandmother prepared similar culinary delights had my taste buds been so satisfied. Since Meyer knew the owners, two colorful characters, Fred Senn and his vivacious wife Helen he introduced us and we liked them immediately. This was to become our new hangout. As we got to know the Senns a little better, we found that we had a lot in common. Fred loved to play chess which was also a favorite pastime of mine; and Helen loved to play bridge, which Ed and I both enjoyed. The four of us became great friends. The Golden Ox also ran a shuttle bus to all the Chicago Bear home football games. They served a champagne brunch before the game with a full dinner after the game. Since I was a big Bear fan, I used this service often. It was a great way to spend time and it took my mind off the stress in my life for a little while. At the end of 1973, Meyer's contract was up and I was on my own. Peter Otto Abeles was flying solo. The world outside my window appeared sunny with no rain in the forecast. I could not see the storm clouds brewing out there beyond the horizon.

* * *

Karla shut her eyes and she felt drops of rain and when she opened them she was sitting on the shoreline of a lake. She vaguely remembered the scenery and then she heard Ernst's voice. "Karla, you are going to freeze." Then he draped a towel around her shoulders. She was in a swimsuit. It was the kind she wore when she would sneak away from her mother's apartment. Ernst snatched her up and carried her under a nearby shelter. They sat and watched the afternoon thundershower come and go; and as the sunshine broke through the scattering clouds, Ernst held her tightly in his arms and kissed her passionately as she closed her eyes again.

CHAPTER XV

*"The block of granite which was an obstacle in
the path of the weak becomes a stepping stone
in the path of the strong."*
Thomas Carlyle

I missed having my mentor Meyer around; and when alone, wished that I was closer to my own father. I dreamed of father and son having long dinners, toasting our successes, and hugging each other as we parted. But it was not to be, now or ever, except in my fantasies as I stared out of my office window.

It was a little scary being in charge of fifty employees, forty of whom worked in the plant and ten were office employees, managers, and clerks. I loved the challenge and the respect I obtained. Paper Recovery was a profitable company from the very beginning, and in a short time we had earned more than the acquisition costs, which was an unexpected coup.

Upper management was ecstatic and gave me continual praise. I spent a lot of time with my new friend and coworker Ed Law. His expertise was with the Paper Mills; and since they were our end customers, that worked in our favor. He patiently taught me the little things that the busy Meyer Lissner was unable to teach me. The details of this business took time and Ed was a willing and able teacher with an amazing sense of humor. I was getting a real education. Ed redefined OTJ (on the job) training with his casual, comfortable approach.

My aging parents were complaining a lot. My father's health continued to worsen and they began asking me to come to New York to visit. My second marriage was continuing to deteriorate. Sandra was drinking excessively late at night, but only after the kids were in bed. She refused to admit that she had a problem and was able to conceal it from her friends. We argued constantly and my response to arriving home each night to a sleeping wife was to work harder and spend even more time away from home. In those days, alcohol abuse wasn't understood and I simply couldn't deal with it. Most evenings I had dinner with Ed to occupy my mind, denying to myself that divorce was inevitable. When the guilt overwhelmed me, I would go home trying to behave like the male images I saw on television shows such as "Ozzie and Harriet" or "Leave It To Beaver." Sandra had a knack for knowing when I had encountered difficulties at work and chose those times to wait up to confront me. She would greet me at the door and begin to rave about my shortcomings, the need for more money, and my work habits. I could not convince her that fewer hours meant less money. She was relentless and after biting my tongue I would fly off into an uncontrollable rage. One night, I stormed out of the house with Sandra nipping at my heels. I bolted for the car, jumped inside and locked the doors. While I sat behind the wheel with my eyes closed, she was still yelling and beating the window with her fists. I started the car, put it in reverse, and began backing out of the driveway while Sandra stepped in front of the car flailing her arms and continuing to scream. I stopped and put the car in neutral while revving the engine. For a brief moment I thought I might put the car in drive and run over her. Then I slowly regained my composure and began crying. I knew then that the chances of our being able to live together again were remote. I backed out into the street and drove sadly away, not looking back, hoping that our children had not witnessed this horrible spectacle. The thought of not being with my children every day sickened me. I suppose I subconsciously chose the only role model I could copy: my father. I vowed to be a provider just like him, the giver of material comforts. I would learn later that my ignorance of emotional support would jeopardize the very children I vowed to protect.

Late one evening, I received a phone call from a pushy investigative reporter with the Madison State Journal. He informed me that Waste Management and I had been indicted by the Dane County Grand Jury for price fixing and wanted to know if I would care to comment. I felt sick and managed a "No comment." I hung up the phone and tried to collect my wandering thoughts. To say I was flabbergasted would have been an understatement. I knew I was innocent but could do nothing until the next morning. I didn't sleep at all the entire night. The following day, I went to our headquarters in Hinsdale to meet with Dean and the company legal staff. I sat in a conference room filled with smartly dressed attorneys, considering the situation. I remember the chatter in the background as I grabbed a glass of water and walked over to the window. Apparently, there is a law in the State of Wisconsin called "one-sided consent." This law allows one person to consent to wire taps of conversations with another person. I was informed that my office and personal phones had been tapped for quite some time and that at least one meeting with my competitor that took place in a drug store coffee shop had been recorded. The purpose of these wiretaps was for my competitor to try to trap me into agreeing to price fixing schemes and bid rigging. I was permitted to listen to some of the tapes. The only thing I ever said was that the competitor's pricing was too low. I never agreed to anything illegal. Everyone at the meeting agreed that the state was really after the corporation and I was just a pawn. I had overcome Nazis, bullies on the south side of Chicago, and a dysfunctional family. I laughed at the absurdity of being snared by the Wisconsin authorities. The decision was made that I should refuse to return to Wisconsin and fight extradition. I know how it felt to be "on the lam." Waste Management was supportive and hired one of the best law firms in Chicago, Jenner and Block, to fight my extradition. It was frightening, but it was out of my control, so I decided to let the attorneys handle the situation and keep my nose to the grind stone.

I could sense that the people at Waste Management did not really understand the waste paper business. At the same time, Ed Law was getting frustrated with the corporate red tape. It wasn't long before my worst fears became a reality. Ed resigned and abruptly left. I felt totally alone. Both of my mentors were gone. Paper Recovery was doing great. Everything else was falling apart. I walked to my office window, downed a highball, and felt that old sense of foreboding once again.

It seems like all bad news comes at night. I was at home trying to spend some quality time with my children when the call came that my father had been rushed to the hospital. I called my brother and made arrangements to meet him in New York. By this time, my father's health had deteriorated to the point where he could no longer work. I felt badly for him and myself for not having known him as a man. His work had kept him going and now it was an uphill struggle to get up in the morning. I wanted to reassure him and let him know that I really cared, but the words would not come. He was in a lot of pain and was quite weak. As we sat at his bedside, it was an awkward situation. Here we were, the Father and his two sons unable to show any real emotion. We were men who had been through an earthly hell together and had made it past that. All we could manage was some small talk, then our father finally expressed his concern about our mother's welfare after his death. We promised to take care of her. As we stepped out of the room to take a break and have a cup of coffee, a doctor told us that my father's case was terminal and we would have to move him to a nursing home. Wow! We had never participated in selecting a place where any of our family would live. Now the two of us would find a home for our father. My brother and I spent the next two days frantically looking for a nursing home that would accept a terminal case. We were like a couple of zombies moving around in a trance-like state performing a gruesome task, finding a place for our father to die. After the second day without finding a suitable place, we got back to the hospital just in time to be with him when he died. My mother was in terrible physical shape and now her emotional state of mind was dangerous. My brother and I were emotionally drained as well. We made the necessary funeral arrangements and notified family members and friends living in New York. The funeral was very small with few in attendance. It was a very sad occasion. I don't know how my brother felt, but I could not understand my state of mind or heart. I am not sure what I was feeling, numbness or nothing. Was there something wrong with me? We stayed a few more days and tried to get my mother situated. She didn't say very much and when she did it was about practical matters. The whole situation was strange. It seemed like Father was away on a sales trip and would return in a week or so. Mother sat in a blue upholstered chair by the curtained window and looked out in silence. I thought to myself, "Yes, Mother. Now you know how it feels to be scared and alone. Keep looking and the hurting will go away." Neither Heinz Robert nor myself could wait to get out of New York. We went to the airport together the next morning, and we talked about many things, but our careers mostly. Neither of us, however, discussed our father's death. It seemed to be the Abeles' way of avoiding pain, by denial. I knew Mother was sitting in that same blue chair. I hoped that she was missing me.

* * *

Karla opened her eyes again and as she looked through the window she said to Peter, "I cannot begin to describe to you, Peter, how lonely one becomes when a part of their life suddenly is taken from them. You expect it from the very beginning of a relationship knowing that one day it will end. But all the planning in the world can never really prepare you, Peter. I was lonely and I was scared and I kept looking but the hurt, it never really went away."

Karla realized she was sitting in her favorite chair and

the box was in her lap. The word on the box was "Yesod." She knew it meant foundation. "Yes, the foundation is the most important part of any structure. Nothing can stand without a foundation." She looked through the window at Peter.

CHAPTER XVI

"What I have lived through I know. What I
am going to live though only God knows."
My Grandmother

The Jewish High Holidays began on September 10 with Rosh Hashanah, the time when we pray for a happy and healthy New Year for our families. This is a time when God opens the book of life, deciding who will live or die, who will or will not have peaceful lives; effectively, his will for mankind.

I had in the past known these things, now I felt these things. I was different but I could not describe all these strange feelings I continued to have. Then during Yom Kippur on September 20, I was saying "Kaddish," my prayer of praise to the Almighty and to the memory of the departed, especially my parents. While at synagogue, sitting in a room full of people, yet all alone, I closed my eyes and this time my mother and father appeared before me. I asked them what was next. They were still silent. I then asked them why for the first time Yom Kippur seemed so meaningful. They were silent. My throat was dry and I felt my hands shaking as I continued my questions.

"I have thought about all the times we were together.

"The last few months I have recalled our past experiences and the circumstances of your deaths. Forgive me when I was not sad, and for the times when I actually felt relief instead of grief. I must ask you, what did I do wrong? Did you ever wish that I were not your son? If you really loved me, why did you hurt me so much? I tried so hard to please you and nothing I did made you happy."

I looked at them through Otto's eyes and they reverently bowed their heads and said a prayer of forgiveness for their sins of the past. Then they slowly faded away and I opened my eyes. Everyone was forgiven. The New Year had begun. I had listened to my dead mother and had boldly decided to finally trust her. God brought us all together here today so that we could finally be a family. I knew that I had much to say to my wife and children.

I told Bonnie I was going to take a walk, and as I did, I thought of the time Ed called me in January of 1975.

He asked me to meet him at The Golden Ox for lunch. He said he had a proposition that I might find interesting. I agreed to the luncheon meeting having no idea what a monumental impact it would have on the rest of my life. Upon arrival, Ed and I greeted like old friends who hadn't seen each other in years. We were seated and after ordering the daily special, Ed got right to the point. He told me that a friend of his was running a large paper mill called the Brown Company. The friend confided in Ed that he was having problems with his purchasing department and asked if Ed would like to start a company to handle all the waste paper purchases for the mill. Ed further explained to me that he was not really interested in trading or buying waste paper and offered to give me 50% of the company if I would do the purchasing. For a minute I was speechless and then I remembered the words of my friend Meyer telling me "Kid, your time will come." Before I could reply, Ed told me to think it over for a couple of days and then get back to him. While returning to my office, I felt as though I were in a daze. There were so many questions and so much information floating around in my head that I could not process all of it. I really wished I could go home like a person with a normal marital relationship and discuss it with my wife. I knew that discussion would be impossible, so as usual I stayed late at the office. Around midnight I headed home and quietly entered.

I was so weary that evening, but I still had too many thoughts whirling inside my brain. It would have been nice to just collapse in my bed and enjoy a night of peaceful sleep. Instead, I tiptoed to my study where I sat down to sort things out. I needed to make some important decisions. As I turned toward the window to look out into the freezing, dark night, I could see my reflection in the glass. The man who appeared before me was a stranger. I had created him to survive in the business world and he was doing a remarkable job there. My alter ego began thinking about what it would be like to own a business. I realized that I would lose all of my stock options and that I might alienate some of the people at Waste Management. But I felt that this was the economic opportunity of a lifetime so it did not make the decision very hard to reach.

I called Ed the next day and told him to count me in. I made an appointment to meet with Dean Buntrock to inform him of my decision. We had a very emotional meeting, both nearly in tears. I thought we had ended our meeting on a positive note. However, after I left the office, he must have had some second thoughts. Late that afternoon, they called me and told me they wanted me to leave my position immediately. I packed my belongings, said goodbye to everyone, and walked out to begin my new job as the co-owner of my own company.

I wasn't sure what I was going to do with the rest of the day. For me, 3:00 P.M. was the middle of the workday and I knew I did not want to go home. I decided to go to the Golden Ox and I called Ed to see if he would join me. I needed a friend and he reassured me that every new beginning in life involved closing some doors. The words sounded good and I felt better until I looked at my watch and decided I should go home. I had delayed that departure for as long as possible. When I got there, Sandra had been drinking and we had a terrible argument. I had so many things going on that I just couldn't take the drinking and arguing any longer. I told her I was moving out the next day. I sat up half the night trying to figure out how things could be so good and so bad at the same time. I also tried to rationalize in my mind that moving out was not the same as running away. No matter how many times I went over it, I could not convince myself as I kept seeing the innocent faces of Bryan and Michelle. I looked at a picture of

Sandra and me when we were first married and I thought of all the dreams we had. I remembered even then when she drank her emotional tolerance was low. I should have recognized it but I didn't. I should have seen that working this many hours and not staying at home could only end up like this, but I only saw business opportunity. I came to realize that I wouldn't be the one to teach my son how to knot his tie, how to shine his shoes, or how to hold a baseball. I wouldn't be the one to tell my daughter how beautiful she looked the first time she made an attempt to apply lipstick and smear it on her face. I wouldn't be the one to admonish her first date when he came to pick her up. I didn't really understand a damn thing about how to keep a relationship together or how to relate to my kids. I realized that there must be a host of other guys just like me. I truly hoped the world would be able to overcome our ineptitude. All the counselors I saw and all the attorneys I consulted were not going to be able to correct this problem.

The next day I moved in with Ed at his apartment. We went over our plan for starting the new business during the next few days. He explained to me that the Brown Company had agreed to advance us a minimum of $50,000.00 so neither one of us had to put in any money for start-up. Fortunately, Ed had more than enough assets for us to establish credit. We rented an office, then ordered stationery and all the necessary forms we would need to start operating.

We realized we had not picked out a name for the new company. We bounced several names around but discarded each of them for one reason or another. Ed started doodling on the legal pad in front of him and he asked me, "What are we in business for?" Before I could answer him, he blurted out, "For Love of Money." This is how the F-L-O-M Corporation was born. We made arrangements to buy my company car from Waste Management and in about two weeks, we were ready for action.

By February, I had left my job, separated from my wife, and become a business owner. It was the same old story. My professional life was rewarding and my personal life was a mess. I could sense my children were unhappy. Every time I went to visit them, there was a confrontation with Sandra and the little time I spent with the kids was not meaningful quality time. Feeling that it was probably too late, I made very little effort to solidify my relationship with the children. Once again, my answer to everything was hard work. I knew how to do that, didn't I, Father?

We had very few start-up problems with the business. All in all, our new venture went well. I handled all of the buying and trading and Ed handled the technical side of the business. The Brown Company was pleased with our performance and I was able to acquire some new customers.

Ed and I had set up an "odd couple" existence in his apartment. He loved to cook and I didn't mind cleaning up. Ed's outgoing personality garnered us a lot of dinner invitations from our neighbors that we never turned down. This made our home life very pleasant. Move over, Tony Randall and Jack Klugman, there were new kids on the block! The only thing wrong with our living conditions was the size of the apartment and the location. This prompted our decision to find a larger place to live. We decided to rent an apartment on the golf course a mile from the office. We leased and furnished the new apartment in one day. In the course of the two years we lived there, we played golf only once and our game was reflective of the amount of time we spent on the course.

Over the next few months, Sandra and I made a feeble attempt to salvage our marriage. As I had expected, our half-hearted attempts failed miserably. I recall driving up to my old house in a pouring rain and seeing both Bryan and Michelle peering out the front window at me. I sat in the car while I gazed at their sweet little faces. Is that the way Otto looked from his window? Must history always repeat itself? Can the cycle ever be broken? I allowed the windows to fog over so the kids wouldn't see me crying just like I never saw my father cry. By the time I got inside the house, Sandra had put them to bed and I never even got to speak to them that night though I can't imagine what I might have said. That night we didn't argue. There was nothing more to say or do. Within a few days, Sandra started divorce proceedings. I didn't contest them, just wanting it to be over.

It was good to know that with all the troubles in my life, Heinz Robert was doing well and getting more and more recognition for his research throughout the academic world. He was shouldering more than his share of the responsibility for our mother's care and she was slowly adapting to being a widow. I couldn't focus on her since all of my time and attention was spent on my goofed-up-middle-aged existence. Then my life was changed.

I was on a buying trip to Maryland when one of my suppliers fixed me up with his ex-sister in law. It was supposed to be a double date; but as fate would have it, the date ended up just Bonnie Asrael and myself. I realized more intensely what a pitiful existence I had been living. Years later, Bonnie told me she could see the loneliness in my face as we were having dinner that first time. The date was wonderful. After dinner, we talked into the wee hours of the morning. After staying up most of the night, I went to work at the usual time. Bonnie and I were going out on another date the second night and I was so tired I fell asleep at the dinner table. She became concerned and shook me asking me if I was alright. I assured her that I was only "love sick" and went back to sleep. Bonnie had a wonderful family of three girls, Debbie, Stacey, and Marilyn, ranging in ages from eleven to fifteen. She also had lovely, doting parents. As I got to know Rose and Sam Asrael, I realized just how wonderful it would be to have parents like hers. They were Orthodox Jews practicing their religion privately and not trying to make anyone in their family change the way they lived their lives. Rose was a warm giving person always ready to help anyone in trouble. You had to be very careful not to admire any objects in her home because chances were that she would try to give it to you or would go out and buy something similar to give to you as a gift. Sam owned a metal plating business and bikers came to him from far and wide due to his honesty and workmanship. I soon learned that even though he did quality work, he never charged enough for it. If someone came to him with no money, he would either let him pay later or possibly not at all. He always treated everyone with respect. He owned the building he occupied and had a renter on the second floor who operated a small printing business. I once asked Sam why he only charged the tenant $10.00 a month and he replied, "It's okay. He gives me a 10% discount on all my printing." Sam was the most charitable man I had ever met. No matter who came to him, Sam would give generously. I am truly thankful that Rose and Sam came into my life and I miss them very much now that they are gone. How strange this was to me that everyone in a family loved each other. Right from the beginning of our relationship, they all accepted me and made me feel welcome. From that time on until I moved to Maryland, I spent almost every weekend with Bonnie and her family. Since I couldn't be with my kids, it was pleasurable to see Bonnie enjoying her children.

My divorce was finally settled and we got an interlocutory decree that would become final in one year. Meanwhile, Bonnie and I were discussing marriage. The idea of marrying Bonnie certainly appealed to me and the Flom Corporation was thriving. However, my legal problems with the state of Wisconsin were ongoing. Every time I took a business trip to Wisconsin, I was worried that I would get picked up by the authorities and taken to Madison to stand trial. I often wondered how Bonnie would feel if a fugitive proposed marriage to her.

My children were sensing that I was contemplating moving to Maryland and that there were new, seemingly more important, people in my life. This made them feel even more threatened and insecure. For children of only twelve and eleven years of age, they were certainly going through some bad times. I just didn't know what to do for them. Hard work and money would not take care of their needs. But I had nothing else to give. I probably hurt the ones that I loved the most. I couldn't blame this one on Mother. This was entirely my own creation. Life, however, was about to bestow a blessing on me that I didn't deserve.

Early in 1977, I relocated the Flom office to Maryland. Since my divorce was not yet final, Bonnie and I decided to live together until we were able to marry. It was wonderful since we had the blessing of her parents as well as her children. It was a new experience for me to be happy at home and at work simultaneously. All at once I had a new family. I learned what it meant to be close with family members, hugging, kissing, and saying "I love you." Bonnie and the girls were my main support group especially when I was having problems with Bryan and Michelle. They were both rebelling in their own individual ways. Bryan was having disciplinary problems in school and Michelle became antagonistic and demanding. I knew in my heart that I ran away when they needed me the most. Guilt and remorse were my constant companions. It was great to know that there were many people who really loved me and whom I loved in return. I wished I could have my children with me, too. I was still trying to see them as often as possible, but our time together was not very comfortable. I was beginning to wonder if there would ever be a time when everything would come together for me, my kids, and our new family. Would all of the problems and sadness ever disappear?

I had just gotten the new Maryland office settled when I got a call from Ed. He wanted to know if I would be interested in buying a folding carton plant in Minneapolis. This proposal sounded challenging and my answer was an emphatic yes. While the negotiations for the new company were still going on, my divorce became final and Bonnie and I got married on August 10. By the end of that year, Ed and I were the proud owners of Flour City Box Co. It was decided that Ed would run the new company and I would continue to manage Flom. Both companies continued to do well. My professional life and my personal life were on track now, except for my deep concerns for my two children.

Then, like a bolt of lightning, the most extraordinary event of my career occurred. By October 1978, the State of Wisconsin's extradition efforts were becoming serious. The case had now reached the Supreme Court of the United States. If my attorney's efforts in the highest court of the land failed, I would be extradited to Wisconsin to stand trial. What had started as a legal nuisance had escalated into an enormous problem. Needless to say, I had visions of myself serving time in a Wisconsin penitentiary. The answer to my problem came in the form of a phone call from Dean Buntrock telling me that the State of Wisconsin was willing to accept a plea of nolo contendere. This pleading does not admit guilt but subjects you to the same punishment you would receive if you had pled guilty. The state had agreed the punishment would only be a fine. My other option was to go to trial and Waste Management would defend me vigorously. It was not hard to come to a decision because I did not want a long, time-consuming trial. I agreed to the plea.

One week later, I flew to Madison with my attorneys and reported to the authorities. When I arrived at the courthouse, I was escorted to a small room next to the courtroom and handcuffed to the chair. I was told that the judge would be in to see me soon. Everyone left the room and there I was alone, shackled to the chair. What a nightmare this was, I was scared to death. I began to have major questions run through my head, such as what if they forgot about me or what if the judge was late? It was horrible.

Then my thoughts took me back in time to the train ride from Vienna to Rotterdam. We were at the Dutch Border and the Nazi authorities were making their last inspection of our papers and baggage. Would they open the smuggled suitcase?

I was interrupted when everyone came back into the room and they released me from the chair and took me into the courtroom. My attorneys entered my plea and the judge levied the fine and told me I was free to go. This transpired within a matter of minutes. My ordeal was finally over and I could not wait to fly home.

I laughed when I thought of Ed as Felix Unger and myself as Oscar Madison and our Odd Couple relationship. I laughed even more when I thought of myself in one of those striped convict uniforms breaking rocks. The Jewish Holidays had been very good this year. I liked this "getting in touch" stuff more each day. At first I felt weird talking about visions and dreams but now they seemed only natural. I found myself whistling Burt Bacharach tunes as I walked back to retrieve Bonnie. I wondered if she could remember the words to *"Do You Know the Way to San Jose?"*

* * *

Karla looked down and noticed that the black box was gone. She knew it would not be back. Then she looked on her hand and there was a word written in her palm. The word was "Shekhinah" and she knew what it meant. It was the presence of the divine. As she looked up there was no longer a glass in the window. It was an opening, an opening for the past and the present. It was for the loved and unloved portions of her life and Peter's life to be reunited. Karla was so thankful that she laughed and laughed. She feared that she might never be able to stop laughing.

CHAPTER XVII

"As Love enters, fear vanishes."
Ernest Holmes

Bonnie and I threw a Thanksgiving celebration at our home this year, inviting our entire family to attend. We had so much for which to be thankful.

I expressed in writing what is so difficult to say aloud. As I sat at my computer, I was reminded of the day after Thanksgiving in 1998 when Heinz Robert and his wife paid us a visit.

Bryan was in town for the holiday and we all talked and laughed. It was to be the last time I would see my brother with full mobility. A few months later, he was suffering from delusions and could not move around without assistance. The Parkinson's disease had taken its toll.

After being diagnosed with the disease in 1987, Heinz Robert had shown his usual tenacity and "grit" by continuing his work publishing a textbook in 1992 called Biochemistry, followed by being a co-recipient of the prestigious Robert A. Welch Award in Chemistry. This award recognizes scientists for their lifelong contributions to basic chemical research that have made significant and positive impacts on the future. Heinz Robert received a sizable sum of money and a gold medallion. As Bonnie and I sat in a small room with eight Nobel Prize winners in attendance, I remembered my brother's comment to me once again, "We can do anything as long as we stick together." I had made my mark in the business world and Heinz Robert had earned a place for himself in the annals of chemical research. As we had our photograph made together in our black tuxedos, I placed my arm around Heinz Robert and told him how proud I was to have him for a brother.

As a young man he was a member of a ski patrol and had worked as a private detective in Chicago. He had always lived life his own special way. This fascinating and brilliant man now faced the pain and mental anguish of this terrible disease with the same courage and integrity that he faced all of the other challenges in his life.

I leaned back in my chair and clasped my hands together around the back of my neck and whispered, "I love you, Bob." It felt good to say it.

I made a list of everyone that I could think of and I said aloud "I love you" to each of them. It didn't matter if they heard me or not, just doing it made me feel great. I finished by telling God that I loved Him most of all.

I had always liked being in control of things on the outside, but now I had discovered that the greatest power comes from within. I was astonished to find that it took my mother's death to enable me to forgive and love everyone in my life, without the need to understand why they did things to displease or sometimes even hurt me.

I thought of how difficult it was to turn the reins of my company over to Lloyd in 1996. He had learned the business quickly since joining the firm in 1987 and while I knew he could handle the job as president and CEO of FLOM Corporation, I had trouble "letting go," so to speak. Bonnie and I first lived in San Diego during the winter months, and I joyously worked part time during the business transition while honing my tennis game. Then we bought a condo in Naples, Florida and I found that not working at all was even more pleasurable. Watching the sunrises and sunsets on the Gulf of Mexico from our condo window provided greater rewards than making business deals. Flom's chairman of the board could generally be found in shorts, a tee shirt, and a pair of sandals during normal business hours.

The three years leading up to my mother's death had been a time to dispose of the clutter that a long business career accumulates. There is something humbling about receiving your very first Social Security payment and recalling the first time you paid into your account was 1941. Fifty plus years of a man's life was expressed in a few figures on a piece of paper. A sense of my own mortality etched itself in my heart that day.

One evening in the fall of 1997, Bonnie and I had just returned home from dining at one of our favorite restaurants. As we walked to our door, I began experiencing chest pains. We called the doctor and he told us to go to the hospital immediately. Bonnie drove me and we went directly to the emergency room. I told them about the pains and they went to work on me right away. They checked my blood pressure, took an EKG, and checked all my vital signs. They found nothing serious but insisted I stay at the hospital overnight for observation. I was released the next day and went to my heart doctor for a complete check-up. After extensive tests, it was determined that I had two blocked arteries. The options were to treat the blockage with drugs or to have angioplasty. I opted for the procedure and it was performed a week later. It was successful and in a few weeks I received a clean bill of health.

Disease attacks you physically, of course, but also emotionally, injecting constant thoughts of fear at the most inopportune moments. I decided that the only way to fight aging was to take an aggressive approach. I continued body building and healthy eating habits, making great strides in my weight lifting program. Eventually I was able to bench press my weight, quite an accomplishment for a guy in his sixties. I still like to keep a tan but learned to apply sun screens when swimming, playing tennis, or golfing. Physically, I was in the best shape of my life, and I now needed to work on my soul.

Bonnie and I spent a lot of time walking on the beach. She took the Sony Walkman and listened to music while I did some solid reflection. I could sense that life was preparing a great lesson for Peter Otto Abeles. In 1999, at sixty-eight years of age my puzzle finally came together. The smallest of pieces not recognizable when lying in a little pile on the table now came to be discernible.

I turned my computer off and went for a snack. All this thinking about Thanksgiving had made me hungry. I sat at my kitchen table and munched on some fruit while looking out the window at a small blue jay that had perched on my back deck. She appeared as though she had just made the first flight of her life. I thought of my daughter Michelle and how she had boldly stepped out of the nest and learned to fly on her own. For my 65th birthday, Michelle wrote a poem to me followed by a beautiful letter describing her innermost feelings. I walked down to my study and found the scrapbook that contained those stirring words, and I reread each line carefully.

Dear Dad,

I am writing this letter to tell you how I felt regarding the divorce between you and Mother and of the many feelings I have had since that time.

I don't remember the exact date of the divorce because it was a fairly uneventful day for me. You were so busy starting the new business that you weren't around very much anyway. Actually, the separation enabled me to have more time with you than I would have had if you had stayed married to Mother. I enjoyed our weekly dinner "date" very much as well as the time we spent together on the weekends. I would like for you to know that I think you and Mother did a great job handling the divorce. I remember the day you both sat me down and explained the separation. You both made it very clear to me that it had nothing to do with Bryan and me and that you loved us very much. Mother told us that you were a wonderful man, but that the two of you could not live together and that we should never blame ourselves. I found it ironic that you told us exactly the same things in regard to our mother. After that, my life went back to the same way it had always been with school, friends, and swimming. At first nothing changed.

As time went by, however, I began to feel the effects of the divorce. I didn't think that I had changed much but my mother and Bryan changed a great deal. They each had their own problems dealing with the divorce; and as a result, became increasingly more difficult to be around. As Bryan's problems worsened, both of you turned your attention to him and I was just left on my own. In the long run, I think this helped make me a stronger person, but at the time it was very frustrating.

Several years later, after you moved to Washington D.C. and married Bonnie, part of me was very happy for you. You deserved happiness and it was clear to me that you and Mother would have never had that happiness. The other part of me was very resentful of your new family. You had a "normal family life" with Bonnie and her three children while I was "stuck" living with my mother and Bryan and their many problems.

I didn't feel very close to you at that time and always felt like an outsider when I went to visit you and your "family." That feeling was not anything that Bonnie, Debbie, Stacey, or Marilyn caused. It stemmed from you. For a long time it was easier to blame the new-comers than to face the fact that it was your personality making me feel this way. It was very hard not to feel angry when at each visit I felt that you were more a part of their lives than you were of mine. This was most clearly exemplified by two major events. The first was the fact that Bonnie's children were at your wedding while I was not even told about the wedding until after the fact. I don't think you meant to hurt my feelings, but that was a pretty major slight as far as I was concerned.

The second event was my Bat Mitzvah. You came in for the event, of course, but you came without Bonnie and stayed at my party for a whole five minutes. It was not so bad until a few months later when Marilyn told me all about her Bat Mitzvah and the party that you attended.

I guess the bottom line was that I felt like I was living in a very difficult situation and you didn't seem to care. When I talked to you about leaving home and maybe attending a private school, you were not receptive to that idea at all. You told me that my mother needed me at home with her. I don't think you realized how unfair that was to me. I was the child, not the mother. You couldn't stay and deal with her problems, yet you expected me to.

Things did get better when I got to high school. As you know, Bryan's problems had escalated to the point that he was no longer living at home. While it was unfortunate, it did help take some of the stress out of my life. It was very hard on Mother, though. It made her feel like a failure and she took that out on me. She also criticized you when she got angry and then blamed me for everything. I know she was doing her best and she tried hard to "make things up to me," but it was not always easy. I will say that no matter what she did, I always knew she loved me and was trying her best. There was just more going on at that time than she was prepared to handle. I don't mean to make it sound as if I had a horrible childhood and adolescence because overall I did not. There were some very good times and I had a wonderful support system in my extended family. Through these years I was a competitive swimmer and for the most part Mother was great. She was one of my biggest cheerleaders in the stands and very rarely missed a swim meet.

I think you found it easier to relate to me after I started growing up. When I was sixteen, I finally started to develop a relationship with you. With Bryan away at school, we spent more time together just talking. Most people would expect me to have a closer bond with my mother, but actually you have had a huge impact on my life.

When I left for college, our relationship went to a new level. You were more involved in my life than you had ever been. When I was at Indiana University those first two years, I remember you coming to Chicago and driving me and all my "stuff" to school. You even carried all those things up to the fifth floor on a 90-degree day with no air conditioning! I guess you were really glad I had a boyfriend and others to help carry everything my sophomore year. When you left me there that freshman year, you told me that you wanted me to enjoy school and not worry about anything else. I really appreciated the fact that you made sure I didn't have to worry about money and that I could just have fun and maybe study a little on the side.

Then when I transferred to Arizona State my junior year, you were supportive of my transfer even if you did think I was transferring to the "country club." I think you were happy to have a nice place to come visit and I really enjoyed you and Bonnie being there, meeting some of my friends and becoming part of my life.

I can remember asking you for things that you quickly responded "no" to. Most of my friends were spoiled and were never told no. I hated you for it then, but I thank you for it now because some of those friends are now having a hard time dealing with the fact that they can't have everything they want.

I appreciated your support when Mother got sick. Because of her brain tumor, it became my job to get her life in order and make many important decisions. You were so good to Mom during that time and made everything much easier for me.

I also want to thank you for your support as my wedding approached. You made sure that everything went the way I wanted it to and provided a good beginning for Steve and me. You and Bonnie are very important in our lives, and I trust that you will continue to be a big part of our future as our family grows.

I am very proud of the fact that I worked hard and became a lawyer. I am also very fortunate to have been lucky enough to marry a wonderful man who is a doctor. We don't have everything we want, but we have a wonderful life. We have more than most people our age. I remember you saying to me that I would appreciate everything a lot more if I did it for myself. I have to admit you were right!

I may not have always liked what you had to say to me or the way you treated me, but there are two things I am now sure of. One is that you do and you always have loved me in your own unique way. You have played a big role in helping me become the person I am today. The other thing that I am sure of is that I do and always have loved you very much!

Love, Your Daughter,

Michelle

"Thanks, Michelle," I whispered, "for the truth." It was refreshing and allowed both of us to start anew. Several years later, Michelle and Steve, her husband a St. Louis physician would become the parents of two handsome little boys, Joshua and Matthew. As I thought about children, I was reminded of Bonnie's daughters. Usually, it's the kids who have to make the adjustments to a new parent in the beginning, but it was I who had to get accustomed to three beautiful girls and their mom working hard to make me feel right at home. I owe so much to Debbie, the eldest daughter, who was an example to her sisters with her kind manner and wonderful sense of humor. It was like the Brady Bunch without the boys. These days I go to the bagel shop where I see Debbie, who is the manager. She prepares my favorite bagel with cream cheese which is loaded with cholesterol and we don't tell Bonnie. Stacey, the middle girl, was the epitome of stability and sweetness. She was the one you could always count on and today her three children, Jenna, Corey, and Jake share their mother's wonderful characteristics, not to mention her good looks. Bonnie, the consummate matchmaker, was enthralled by our handsome young waiter at the Capitol Center where the Washington Bullets play basketball. Later, while vacationing in the Catskills, it just so happened that the same young man was our waiter there as well. Bonnie arranged a meeting between Stacey and our waiter Lloyd, who were both students at the University of Maryland living in the same apartment complex. Little did I know that her intuitive powers would land us both a son-in-law and the future president of Flom Corporation.

The baby of the family, Marilyn, is a beautiful divorced mother of three lovely children, Hannah, Lauren, and Danny. She has her work cut out for her. While making a point of seeing her mom on a frequent basis along with her other sisters she demonstrates the kind of relationship I wish I had been able to have with my mother. On Marilyn's thirty-fifth birthday this year, I received a special present from her in the form of this beautiful, unexpected note,

It doesn't matter
Marilyn Wood

The common phrase "actions speak louder than words" is thought provoking when I reflect upon the past twenty-two years with Pete, my stepfather. While he is a man of few words, I have come to realize that it doesn't matter because it is truly one's actions that carry the most weight. I would describe Pete's actions as his greatest attribute in that he unconditionally cares and gives deeply in his own quiet way. All that he really asks in return for the help he offers is that I lead a productive and happy life.

Sometimes I joke and say that one would think that Pete had a "cake life," for why else would he become so irate over something as nonsensical as needing to redial a phone number because his call didn't go through the first time? How could a man whose been through so much be so bothered by something that trivial? To this day, I have not been able to figure this out. What I can say is that the meaning behind the behavior no longer concerns me, as does not the behavior itself. One of the perks of being an adult is being able to see things more abstractly than before. Through this maturation process, I have discovered that, in the scheme of things, Pete's absurdities are a small price to pay for having him in my life. Therefore, I've learned to be unaffected by his eccentricities and at times, even humored.

Whenever I hear Natalie Merchant sing "Kind and Generous" on the radio, I immediately think of my mother and Pete. The two of them collectively have saved my life so many times, both emotionally and financially. I sometimes wonder how a man who has overcome so many obstacles in his life could be so incredibly filled with wisdom, honor and character. Again, I suppose the answer to that is "it really doesn't matter how."

The word "stepfather" holds a different meaning for each individual. In spite of the reality that step-families are generally more challenged than biological parent/child relationships, for me, the word "stepfather" does not bear a negative connotation. I would not feel any more connected to Pete if it were his blood running through my veins. It doesn't matter that he is only my "stepfather" because in this context, "only" is "everything" to me. It's ironic that I sit here tonight, on my thirty-fifth birthday, reflecting back on my life and thinking of a conclusion to this paper. While I view my life as having been a difficult journey thus far, I become cognizant that this, too, does not matter. When I put everything in perspective, realizing that some troubled times have passed and some can be conquered, I can focus on that which is really important. The important part of my life is the loving, meaningful relationships. I can proudly say that there is no one more dear to my heart than that boy at the window, my stepfather, Peter Otto.

I had recently spoken with a rabbi friend of mine. He asked why Bryan didn't come into my business. The first-born son in the Jewish tradition has that special birthright. I suppose both Bryan and I know the answer to the rabbi's question. I replied that Bryan marches to the beat of a different drummer. Recently, to my amazement, we have discovered that we share much more in common than either of us would ever have believed. The same stubbornness that prevented us from talking when we should have during those tumultuous years of adolescence and eventually put many miles between us has become that aspect of his personality that I have grown to admire. I encouraged him to join the Army as I remembered how a stint in the military had initiated my transformation into manhood. My father, many years earlier, had been subjected to his father's idea of becoming a man through extreme hard work and unyielding discipline. I now know that the part of him I tried to change is what makes Bryan unique and interesting. After he left the Army he went back to Chicago and began following The Grateful Dead. He traveled all over the country and being the gregarious guy that he is, made many friends. His "deadhead" days resulted in the acquisition of several tattoos and while they generally evoked feelings of negativity for me, Bryan found them to be an expression of freedom. This contradiction to the meaning of tattoos that I had always associated with enslavement based upon my Holocaust memories has been a hard pill to swallow. But I am learning to call them works of art as Bryan often does. Surprisingly, after admiring an earring he wore while visiting us, I, on a dare, had my own ear pierced and occasionally wear one myself. He could not believe it when I visited him and showed up at the door in a French beret and diamond stud. I shudder to think what my mother would have said if she couldn't even handle my sister in law Barbara, in blue jeans! Bryan has carved out a new life for himself in the picturesque state of Oregon. He loves to bike, camp, and is an expert on fine wines. Most of all, he is an adoring father. His precious daughter Jasmine Sequoia is as energetic and outgoing as her father. Bryan has a heart for the downtrodden of society and while our politics are generally in disagreement, I respect his sensitivity. He is a much better father than I was at that age and for that I praise him. On a business trip to the West Coast, I took a few extra days to accompany Bryan on a hike in the Cascade Mountains. After walking for several hours, we stopped to have lunch and Bryan commented that he could smell the sweet aroma of marijuana. A few seconds later, we heard giggling and after walking up the trail a few feet, we saw a group of people skinny-dipping in a mountain stream. Bryan looked at me as if to offer a challenge. I don't know what possessed me, but I felt an overwhelming desire to show Bryan that his father was "hip." I immediately threw off my tee shirt and flung my jeans over a tree branch and placed my hiking boots on a rock. I have to admit I didn't remove my BVD's until I was very close to the water in case I had to make a quick exit. When my ungirded loins came in contact with that cold mountain water, I screamed loudly and found myself frolicking naked among strangers. Bryan and I laughed together as we never had before. I think while I will never be able to replace those years when he needed me most as a father, perhaps for the remainder of my life he can be my friend.

When I started counting my many blessings, it became clear to me that they were as numerous as the stars in the sky. This was going to become a new hobby of mine, thanking God for every single blessing of life.

CHAPTER XVIII

Relax. Listen. God is with you right here.
Right now.
Excerpt from the book Ground Zero

I returned to my computer and prayed that I could write the appropriate words to express how I felt. I had to tell Michelle and everyone else in my life about my experiences. A voice from within me urged me to write everyone in my family a letter. After all it was a simple letter that my father had written that saved my young life. I had never considered myself to be a writer, so I picked up the telephone and called Tom Hicks, a close friend and business associate, who had written and published a book with two friends called Ground Zero, which is about everyone's personal search for God. I asked him why he had decided to write a book and he said that one day the idea seemed to just pop into his head and the heads of his two friends at almost exactly the same time. I told him about the voice I heard, not even a voice really, more like a gut feeling. He said very matter of factly, "That's God." I laughed and he sensed my skepticism.

"How else would God talk to you except through your feelings and experiences?" I pondered the question for a moment, then thanked Tom and hung up.

I cracked my knuckles, shook my head from side to side, muttered "What the heck?" and started writing whatever came into my mind.

From the Desk of Peter Otto Abeles

Dear Family,

Bonnie and I are having our annual Thanksgiving celebration. It will be a good way to kick off the new millennium and to get Bonnie to cook. I've just got to let each one of you, in my family, understand how much I love you. It has taken me decades of experiences, both good and bad, to find out who I am and I have a gift for you in the form of twelve life lessons I had to learn, sometimes the hard way.

1. *Accept yourself* and receive the greatest gift ever offered to you, your own life; never letting difficult circumstances or powerful people take control of you.

2. *Believe in yourself* and have confidence that you can do anything your heart desires, then do it.

3. *Define yourself* and detach from the mistakes of the past, remembering that even the most painful events will pass with time.

4. *Engage yourself* and use your own experiences for they are the only possessions you have.

5. *Heal yourself* and mend the spirit of those destructive words and actions that others have imposed upon you.

6. *Immerse yourself* and absorb all that life offers including its demands for all of your energy and abilities.

7. *Know yourself* and realize that shortcomings are part of your learning process.

8. *Market yourself* and remember that you are selling the world on a very special product!

9. *Open yourself* and let the light of day expose the dark places where fear still resides.

10. *Nudge yourself* and sense the gentle push toward courage and opportunity.

11. *Pardon yourself* and release the playful child held prisoner by all the yesterdays that stifled your imagination and creativity.

12. *Love yourself* and enjoy the fact that what you think about every little thing is very important to me.

We will expect you at 4:00PM and you are to stay no later than 10PM as we will no doubt be very tired from entertaining all the grandchildren.

Sincerely yours (even when I screw up),

Otto

It was a wonderful Thanksgiving celebration. Everyone attended except for Heinz Robert and his wife. The disease had taken its toll and he was not able to make the trip. I was very disappointed because it had meant so much to me when he had visited our house the previous Thanksgiving. I now knew that he would not be seeing me this year in Florida.

Chapter XIX

Dignity does not consist in possessing honors,
but in deserving them.

Aristotle

In December, when Bonnie and I prepared to leave for our vacation home in Florida, I was saddened to hear that Heinz Robert was no longer able to travel. At that point, he required twenty-four hour a day medical care. By January, of the new millennium, Heinz Robert had long periods when the powerful drugs that were given to control the tremors caused him to hallucinate. To see this man, my brother, who had a mind like a steel trap reduced to almost a vegetable-like state was so depressing for his family and for me. His greatest burden, I believed, was the realization that he would no longer be able to do all the things he loved.

In March, the family wanting some degree of normalcy in their lives, decided to take Heinz Robert to dinner at one of his favorite local restaurants. The evening ended up in disaster as he began flailing his arms uncontrollably and the family had to leave in the middle of dinner to take him home. I received a phone call from his wife informing me of the incident; and after I hung up, I began to accept the inevitability that Heinz Robert would not be with me much longer.

Miraculously, some time in April there were some on-again, off-again moments when Heinz Robert was lucid. I was able to catch him in one of those moments once by telephone, and we had a meaningful conversation for several minutes. This would be the last time I would be able to talk to my brother.

About a month later, I received a phone call that Heinz Robert was in the hospital with pneumonia and was refusing to eat. Deep in my heart I knew this was the beginning of the

151

152 / Otto, the Boy at the Window

end, however I refused to accept it. I tried to talk to him on the phone several times but he wouldn't speak to me, so I flew to Boston to see him. He acknowledged my presence, his eyes followed me wherever I roamed in his room, but he did not want to, or perhaps could not, have a conversation. He continued to refuse to eat, hallucinated often, and talked to other family members of not wanting to go on. I remember kissing him on the forehead when it was time to leave that day. As he lay there, it occurred to me that this was the first time I had kissed him since we were children, nearly sixty years earlier.

In the first week of June, I received a call from my sister-in-law and my niece Lisa, asking that I come back to Boston to have a meeting. I flew there the next day, and we had a family meeting at the hospital. Robert's daughter, his son, his personal physician, and my sister-in-law listened as the doctors explained to us that intravenous feeding would not supply the calories that were needed to fight the pneumonia and to sustain life. Their solution was to put in a feeding tube, but this was an invasive procedure and would require surgery. Without this procedure, Heinz Robert would die. We agreed unanimously not to allow the surgery. This was Heinz Robert's wish, and even though we all left the meeting with heavy hearts, we complied with his desires.

As I flew back to Washington, I thought about my mother's death. Thank God she died first and did not have to witness her first-born's death. Two weeks later, I got the call that my dear brother had passed away just a little over a year after our mother died. This time, my feelings were opposite from the impressions I had about her death. My brain told me he was better off and his suffering was over, but my heart was aggrieved because I loved him so much. I felt compassion for his wife and children. I knew that I had to be strong because they needed me. I thanked God for the support of Bonnie and all our children. Once again, everyone rallied around me to show how much they loved me. I felt really lucky to be cherished by so many people.

That same day Bonnie and I flew to Boston again. After

checking into our hotel, we went to Heinz Robert's house to visit with Barbara and the children. Bonnie, Lisa, her husband George, and I went to the funeral home to make the arrangements. Barbara was too distraught to go, so Steven, their son, stayed with her. We set the funeral for Tuesday afternoon and called on an old colleague and friend of Heinz Robert's, the rabbi emeritus, from Brandeis University. Rabbi Al Axelrod was retired but readily agreed since he was so fond of Heinz Robert.

When Tuesday arrived, we couldn't have asked for a better day. It was sunny and warm, and as we rode in the limo with Barbara and some close friends, I was flooded with emotions.

I was the only survivor of the Abeles family who made that trek from Vienna across the Atlantic so many years before. It was a sobering thought. So much time had elapsed since we walked the decks of the S. S. Rotterdam and my "scientific advisor," my thirteen-year old brother, taught me about the ocean and the stars. Now, according to Jewish tradition, I would cast a shovel full of dirt on his lowered wooden casket. My emotional state at the time would not allow me to speak at the service, though there were many thoughts I would have liked to have shared. I was, however, pleased when I learned that Lisa, perhaps the person who knew Heinz Robert the best, was prepared to impart some intimate feelings about her father. When she stood up looking so pretty in her sun dress, I was reminded of the picture on the mantle in Heinz Robert's house of him doting over his little girl, when her soft voice, quivering with emotion, filled the summer afternoon.

"A couple of years ago, I remember trying to discuss retirement with my father. Dad said Brandeis and my work are my life. You can't retire from it.

My father's intellectual world was his life, and from my early childhood he was my teacher as much as my father. Each night at dinner, I was grilled on what I had learned at school that day, what were my handouts and homework assignments. I endeared myself to less competent teachers, after a lesson at home, by raising my hand with comments like 'That isn't actually how photosynthesis works.'

My father made me a bright red board with wires behind it and questions and answers to math problems on the front. When I put one wire on a question and the other on the correct answer, a lightbulb at the top of the board lit up. I loved making that lightbulb glow!

When new math came along and colored sticks replaced multiplication tables, my dad took me up to his study and drilled me on those tables saying sternly, 'and no fingers.' But he made it clear that learning wasn't about rote memorization. He taught me that it was the foundation, but only the foundation, for the fun stuff—Thinking! My dad gave me many of the tools that I need to both think and live with.

1. *Estimate the answer.* This was more than an approach to word problems. It was an approach to life. Life is not a formula. It's about understanding the essence. Once you grasp that, what follows is easy.

2. *Why not "A"?* When I came home with an "A-" my Father would say "Why not "A"?" He didn't mean that he didn't love or support me for not getting an "A." He wanted me to expect the best out of myself and for myself and to never settle. I've taken that lesson and applied it to school, my work, and most importantly, my choice of husbands. He is the best life has to offer.

3. *Make mistakes* (Or anything worth doing well is worth doing badly) This lesson about learning is also about trust. My dad, aka "The Ayatolla," didn't make behavioral rules in my adolescence. I had no curfew, no structures on discipline, or who were my friends. I am sure I made mistakes in judgement. But both my par-

ents knew that they raised me with values and with love and that in the end, I would get it right. People who you look up to need to show you trust before you learn to trust yourself.

My father's life of research and teaching was seamless with his life at home. No wonder he couldn't retire. That was why in planning a "family funeral" that family had to include his family of colleagues and students when the lesson books were put away, and the card table came out on weekends. You were the people he talked about. Dr. Westheimer, as his true mentor, people like JoAnne Stubbe, for her intelligence and determination and people like Bill Jencks, about whom he said with pride, "He's smarter than me."

On behalf of my family, I'd like to thank you all for coming here today. It is meaningful that his loss is being recognized by the very people who were the core of his life—the friends and family who loved him and the colleagues who shared his passion in life. Thank you all."

As I watched Lisa talk about her father, I looked around and I was amazed by how many people were in attendance. There were colleagues, ex-students, friends, and renowned scientists. It made me feel good to see how many people cared. Before the services, I talked with Rabbi Axelrod and he told me he had known my brother for many years and that during that time they had carried on countless discussions regarding different subjects. He said that every encounter ended with my brother saying "You're nothing but a left-wing liberal." I chuckled remembering that one of Heinz Robert's most endearing qualities was his brutal honesty.

When the rabbi rose to speak at the services, he told of many wonderful things Heinz Robert had done, most of which I was unaware, including establishing the first Jewish Sunday School for kids at the university. This gregarious, ruddy-faced character in a straw plantation hat, looking like an ex-college linebacker, raved on for thirty minutes about the positive characteristics of my brother. I was beaming with pride after hearing of his accomplishments.

Bonnie and I flew home that night, and a couple of days later I got a telephone call from Barbara telling me she had received over two hundred cards and letters from Heinz Robert's friends, associates, and ex-students from around the world. I took out a picture that was made at my house when Heinz Robert visited in 1998. I placed it side by side with the picture of us as young boys at our vacation home in Austria in 1936. My mind transcended to the time, after my mother had scolded me severely at the dinner table and I lay in my bed crying, Heinz Robert came to me and spoke to me in his gentle voice. "The world is ours to conquer, Otto. Nothing will stop us as long as we stick together. Goodnight my dear, sweet brother." I paused, with tears in my eyes and quietly whispered, "Goodbye, Heinz Robert." I knew now how prophetic those words really were. We needed each other then and we did conquer the cruelest of worlds, but only because we did stick together. We both found a world outside our windows where real love existed. I thanked Heinz Robert for living up to his end of the bargain and it was now up to me.

* * *

Karla was looking at another picture. It was a picture of herself with her two baby boys and she was thinking. "I am so proud. I'm so proud of my boys. Aren't you, Ernst?"

"I certainly am, Karla, and did you hear the good news? Our grandchild, Lisa, is going to have a baby. Heinz Robert will be so proud. I better go, now, darling," Ernst said as he kissed her lightly then turned away. "Are you coming?"

"No, you go ahead. I think I'll just be alone with Otto for a few minutes."

CHAPTER XX

*"We must laugh at man to avoid
crying for him."*
Napoleon Bonaparte

I can't begin to tell you how warm and beautiful my memories had suddenly become, filled with humor and joy instead of pain and fear. I took the rest of the afternoon off, thinking of all the wonderful experiences that flooded my mind.

I began recalling the dry sense of humor my father had during my boyhood days in Vienna. He would respond to a question he didn't necessarily want to answer by saying, "Ask the horse." I suppose this practice went back to the days when horse-drawn carriages were prevalent on the city streets. Prior to the Anschluss in Vienna, I was walking down the street with my father when we were approached by a boy of about ten. As he ran up to my father, he said, "Hey, mister, what time is it?" My father answered, "Ask the horse." The boy answered, "I am!" My father was at first, shocked, then all three of us started laughing.

My brother's sense of humor from an early age was questionable to say the least. His dark humor started when he paid me to stick my tongue out at Mother when her back was turned. For this, I got a lousy penny. The risk was not worth the beating I received when I got caught, which was more often than not.

Later in Chicago, while he was in charge of the physics section of the Museum of Science and Industry, he dressed a mechanical robot in red checkered underwear and rigged its trousers to fall during the middle of the demonstration, causing quite an uproar. Even after the onset of his disease, he never missed an opportunity to "get" me. While touring Heinz Robert's campus at Brandeis University, Bonnie and I

157

were shown the chapel. A group of people came out of the chapel after a wedding ceremony and saw us standing there contemplating use of the building. One of the ladies, smiled and asked "Are you planning a wedding here?" My brother solemnly answered, "No, I'm planning my funeral." The lady was speechless and turned away. Bonnie later said that she thought she saw tears.

I'm afraid that same wry sense of humor lives in me. I was working at the main library at the University of Chicago at the "Returns" desk. There was a big slot where people could drop the books they wanted to return. One night I climbed into the container designed to catch the books at the bottom of the return slot. I sat in the container and waited for some unlucky party to drop a book. Two nuns came in together and one dropped a book into the slot and I slowly pushed it back out onto the floor. Three times the nun picked up the book and dropped it back into the slot. Finally, I stuck my arm through the slot and said, "I'll take that book, please." She screamed and ran out the door.

Ed Law, my partner, is the most unpretentious human being that I have ever met. He is oblivious to style and brand names. One day in Chicago, Ed and I had an appointment with an executive of one of the large paper mills. He was to pick us up at the office of Paper Recovery. When he pulled up to the front door, we got into the large, shiny car with him and after we had been driving for about ten to fifteen minutes, Ed, who didn't know very much about automobiles, said, "Hey, this is a real nice car. What model is it?" It turned out that we were riding in a brand new Rolls Royce. The owner didn't say a word, but just looked at Ed with a puzzled expression on his face. I whispered to Ed that it was a Rolls Royce worth over $150,000. Ed shrugged his shoulders and simply replied, "Oh."

Even my divorces had a funny twist I thought as I reflected on an ancient tradition. According to the Jewish religion, one cannot remarry without having a Jewish divorce that is called a "Get." The Orthodox Jewish religion is chauvinistic and it therefore makes it easy for a man to divorce but very hard for a woman to do so. I had heard that if a man demands a Jewish divorce and the ex-wife refuses to sign the appropriate papers, a group of Rabbis can go to the woman's house and place the paperwork in her donkey's saddlebag or cooking pot. So when Sandra's families' Rabbi demanded a Jewish divorce, I wrote a letter to my ex-wife, Meryl. I told her that if she did not sign the appropriate papers, all of the Rabbi's in the city of Los Angeles would descend upon her house and place the papers either in her donkey's saddlebag or her cooking pot. She laughed at the thought of that sight, immediately signed and returned the papers to me.

I learned the secret of staying young when I was chosen to fill the final slot in a golf foursome at my Club. At sixty eight, my age (not my golf score) I was known to the other players as the young "starker" which means "strong kid." The ages of the other three vary from eighty five to eighty nine. Most of the lunch time conversations were about the roaring twenties and early thirties. Recently, Jack Gorden, one of the foursome, passed away. As Bonnie and I watched and listened to the host of friends and loved ones eulogizing my golf partner, I became more convinced that nothing in this life matters as much as the love and appreciation of a man's family.

"Jack, I'm going to miss you a lot," I thought to myself realizing how much I had always wanted the adoration this man had received.

The stories kept coming into my head and I laughed and cried all afternoon. I don't know why it has taken me a lifetime to learn how to reconcile myself with the places, people and experiences of my past, thus allowing me to clearly interpret the real and far deeper meanings, but that is just the way it is. I have ceased trying to figure it all out which is a tremendous waste of valuable time and have chosen instead to live the balance of my life by the wisdom of Bonnie's handmade message prominently displayed on her dressing table. "Stop and smell the roses." Every morning when I rise and turn to stare out my window, I see the rising sun and I am so happy to be here on this big round green and blue sphere. I feel Bonnie's warm hand touching my back and Otto and I know that we are not alone.

*   *   *

"No, Peter, you are not alone and you will never be alone. That was my mistake. I didn't realize that." Karla stood and she felt a presence. It was a beautiful presence and she felt a warmth that she had never felt before in her life. She turned and there was a dazzling light and a radiance. Out of that radiance there appeared a tiara encrusted with diamonds. She took it and on the tiara was written a word, Keter. "Ahh, yes," she said. "I've been waiting for this." For Keter meant crown. She placed the crown upon her head and walked toward the radiance. Before she was engulfed by it, she turned and saw the opening, the window, slowly close and she smiled. She would be seeing Peter soon enough, but for now he was doing just fine.

EPILOGUE

The ten beautiful Hebrew words that Karla is given and ultimately comes to understand have a rich tradition in Jewish mysticism. While they are separate words, they are part of the unity of all things. Everything that happens in our lives is essential in providing us an opportunity to understand the infinite. Those ten beautiful words describe the ten divine attributes called the Sefirot and allow for an individual to constantly receive the jewels of the universe as described in Ezekiel 28. "Every precious stone adored you, ruby, topaz and emerald, chrysolite, onyx and jasper, sapphire, turquoise and beryl. Your settings and mountings were made of gold on the day you were created." Tom and I sincerely hope that you will receive your treasure box filled with priceless jewels that may sometimes puzzle you, disturb you, but are guaranteed to assist you as you seek to understand this beautiful thing called you. Like Otto and I discovered, it's very hard to think eternal when you are worried about how you are going to make it through the day. If you will learn to be thankful and learn to forgive, then and only then will you be able to receive the wisdom (KABBALAH) that great men throughout the ages have sought. There is no reason to wait until tomorrow for the things you truly want because they are waiting for you today.

Peter Otto Abeles lives in Maryland. Tom Hicks, co-author of *Ground Zero*, is a lecturer and speaker on spirituality in modern America. He lives in Tennessee.